CRYPTOCURRENCY TRADING STRATEGIES FOR BEGINNERS

LEARN TECHNICAL & FUNDAMENTAL ANALYSIS,
MARKET PSYCHOLOGY, MONEY MANAGEMENT + DAY
& SWING TRADING TIPS FOR BITCOIN & ALTCOINS

DIGITAL INVESTOR HUB

D1714412

investing. We are not responsible and take no responsibility for the investments you make, these are your decisions."

Created with Vellum

CONTENTS

SPECIAL BONUS!

Want Our Handbook For Free?

Get **FREE**, Unlimited Access to it and all of our new books by joining the Fan Base!

Scan W/ Your camera to Join!

I

CRYPTOCURRENCY DAY TRADING FOR BEGINNERS

INTRODUCTION

The cryptocurrency world is changing rapidly, and this book will cover all the aspects regarding investing and trading cryptocurrencies. Bitcoin, Ethereum, ICOs, blockchain technology, and cryptocurrency trading are the newest hot topics today. Cryptocurrencies and blockchain technology will alter how we see the world. This book aims to enhance your cryptocurrency trading and investment skills.

You have most probably heard about Bitcoin, and it is likely why you are reading this now. Cryptocurrencies have made thousands of headlines, and there are many tales of people who have accumulated vast wealth, and others have made substantial losses by investing in crypto.

Everybody has their stance when it comes to cryptocurrencies. Some people are in complete favor of them, while others are quite the opposite. We have seen many investment professionals predict the rise and fall of Bitcoin prices. Is Bitcoin a secure, reliable long-term investment? How can you get your hands on one safely and minimize the risks involved? What does all this even mean?

Crypto assets are remarkable because it is a revolution by the people in the financial world. Almost every other technology in the financial realm was introduced by big banks who collected most of the profits and left remains for the retail trader, alongside regular traders (you and me). However, in today's world, you and I can easily make huge profits as the big banks watch from the sides as they have no control over Bitcoin and other cryptocurrencies.

Famous Bitcoin quotes by famous people

Bitcoin's parabolic rallies have spurred a lot of interest in the cryptocurrency sector triggering reactions from prominent players over the years. Influential people have joined the debate, and they have provided their input on the revolution. Bitcoin conversations have drawn both fierce supporters and harsh critics as well. Some of the most famous people to comment about Bitcoin and cryptocurrencies include:

1. *"Bitcoin is a remarkable cryptographic achievement and the ability to create something*

that is not duplicable in the digital world has enormous value." – **Eric Schmidt** (CEO Google)

2. *"We have elected to put our money and faith in a mathematical framework that is free of politics and human error."* – **Tyler Winklevoss** (Co-founder Gemini)

3. *"Virgin Galactic is a bold entrepreneurial technology. It's driving a revolution and Bitcoin is doing just the same when it comes to inventing a new currency."* – Sir Richard Branson (Founder of Virgin group of companies).

4. *"It's money 2.0, a huge huge huge deal."* – **Chamath Palihapitiya** (Previous head of AOL instant messenger).

5. *"You can't stop things like Bitcoin. It will be everywhere and the world will have to readjust. World governments will have to readjust."* – **John McAfee**.

6. *"Bitcoin is a techno tour de force."* – **Bill Gates**.

Crypto riches

Digital currencies eliminate the need for middlemen, extra cost, and wastage of time. Most importantly, many people have created vast amounts of wealth investing and trading digital assets. The founders of various founders of these cryptocurrency projects get rich from their projects and those who are bold enough to get involved in them during these early stages.

Many new traders choose to jump in with both feet without conducting sufficient research. Even though this approach will help you understand the basics of cryptocurrency trading, it is still risky and pretty reckless. This book will explain to newbies and rookie traders the essential elements of cryptocurrency trading, detailing particular factors that every trader should know.

If you are new to Bitcoin and have zero technical knowledge or trading experience, this book will help you master buying, selling, cryptocurrency trading, Bitcoin, and Ethereum profitably. This book will explain the basics of Bitcoin, blockchain, Ethereum, and cryptocurrency trading step-by-step and guide beginners into buying their first-ever Bitcoin from anywhere across the globe.

Besides, you will learn how to set up a Bitcoin wallet, conducting technical and fundamental analysis before investing in a coin, trading altcoins, portfolio management, technical analysis tools, and the mistakes to avoid when trading cryptocurrencies. This book will guide you on how to PROFIT from the fastest growing market in the world.

My experience in trading goes long back before the invention of Bitcoin, and it has not been an easy ride. There have been victories and tragedies along the way, but for the better part, I underwent tragedies while learning the trade. As you read through the book, you will find out that these many botch-ups taught me essential lessons. Lessons that each and every trader and aspiring traders should be aware of. Fortunately for you, you don't have to undergo the same self-inflicted pain I went through because I will pass those crucial lessons to you.

I will walk you through the tricks, tips, and tools to become a successful cryptocurrency trader. We will detail the steps of opening a trading account, how to create a wallet, researching cryptocurrencies through technical and fundamental analysis, and opening and closing positions. I will guide you on the factors to consider before selecting a crypto wallet and before joining a trading platform or exchange.

Moreover, I will reveal all the cryptocurrency websites that I utilize to edge over other crypto traders. You will learn the various trading techniques, choose when to buy or sell, technical and fundamental analysis, and money management skills. After reading the entire book, I dare you not to become wealthy. Cryptocurrencies are the future of finance and investments. I hope you enjoy the ride.

1

A GENERAL VIEW ON CRYPTOCURRENCY

THE EMERGENCE OF DIGITAL CURRENCIES

Technologists first implemented the earliest version of cryptocurrencies following a night theft at a petrol station. Onwards, the petrol station asked customers to buy from them using smart cards rather than money.

Fast forward to the early 1980s, David Chaum came up with a cryptographic concept for digital money called "Blinded Cash." The computer scientist explained people could exchange digital money anonymously by using a blind digital signature. This signature would change hands securely without banks having the ability to view or track down users. It's upon this concept that the idea of encrypting money came to be and laid the foundations of digital currencies. Then the internet began to take root approaching the early 90s. Chaum's concept gave birth to web-based payment systems such as PayPal and e-gold. PayPal allowed users to send or receive money through an email form. Several companies did ponder the idea of trading assets through web browsers, and a few individuals even went on to trade gold digitally via the internet.

The rise of e-gold, for instance, enabled individuals to access credit by trading precious metals. But like most trending technologies, the business was plagued with scams. And by 2005, the government began to place bans across web-based trading platforms. But the closest implementation of digital currencies was B-Money. A developer named Wei Dai introduced an electronic cash system that integrated digital pseudonyms and operated within a distributed environment. Like today's decentralized network, the distributed environment enforced contracts without intervention by third parties. While the project never turned out successful, Satoshi Nakamoto - the inventor of Bitcoin, used most of B-Money's features to create the original bitcoin network.

In 1998, Nick Szabo would also create a decentralized virtual network and digital currency called Bit Gold. Most people call Bit Gold the precursor of the Bitcoin network. There were allegations that Nick Szabo could even be Satoshi

Nakamoto owing to the similarities between Bit Gold and Bitcoin's protocols. However, Nick Szabo denied the claims.

In October 2008, a pseudonymous person posted a paper entitled Bitcoin: A Peer-to-Peer Electronic Cash System to a mailing forum discussing the concept of cryptography. The author called himself Satoshi Nakamoto, and his identity has remained a mystery to date. This paper discussed how to implement a peer-to-peer network and use it to conduct payment transactions without the need for trust. In January, Satoshi Nakamoto released the Bitcoin network and mined the first bitcoin block, the genesis block/block number 0. With every block mined successfully, the bitcoin network releases a block reward. This block reward ensures the supply and circulation of bitcoins into the financial ecosystem. With genesis block, Satoshi Nakamoto was rewarded with 50 Bitcoins.

The Early Adopters

In its initial days, the first adopters were primarily computer scientists interested in cryptography and fintech. Hal Finney, a computer engineer and cryptographic activist became the first contributor to the bitcoin network. The engineer downloaded Bitcoin's software on the first day of its release, and Satoshi Nakamoto rewarded him with 10 Bitcoins.

According to this Wiki, other subsequent early adopters were Nick Szabo and Wei Dai. Both had a good history in revolutionizing encrypted money and had launched B-Money and Bit Gold, respectively. Nakamoto remained a mystery before and after actively getting involved in Bitcoin in the first few years. He is estimated to have mined over 1 million bitcoins. After retiring from the bitcoin network, Gavin Andresen became Bitcoin's lead engineer and the Bitcoin Foundation head.

The Bitcoin Foundation is a nonprofit organization that came into being in September 2012 as a means to restore Bitcoin's reputation following numerous scams and scandals. This organization's primary role was to promote Bitcoin and is funded through grants from businesses dependent on Bitcoin technology. The Bitcoin Foundation shares a similar model with the Linux Foundation.

In the first days, Bitcoin's value was determined on the Bitcoin forum. The first marketplace transaction involved the purchase of two pizzas using 10,000 Bitcoins.

Satoshi Nakamoto: The Unknown Creator of Bitcoin

Over the years, journalists and intelligence have attempted to establish the real identity of Satoshi Nakamoto. The New Yorker conducted an investigation that brought up two possible individuals who could be the mysterious bitcoin creator: Vili Lehdonvirta and Michael Clear. Fast Company, a print and online magazine focused on business and technology, linked Bitcoin to an encryption patent application filed by three inventors, Neal King, Charles Bry, and Vladimir Oksman. According to Adam Penenberg's article on Fast Company, "The Bitcoin Crypto-Currency Mystery Reopened," the patent application shared common wording with Bitcoin's whitepaper. However, the trio went ahead and denied the allegations.

Another hoax appeared online of the Australian scholar Craig Wright who allegedly claimed he was Satoshi Nakamoto. While the scholar did not respond to inquiries into the matter, a cybersecurity expert hacked into Craig's email account and established Satoshi Nakamoto as a joint pseudonym for both David Kleiman and Craig Wright.

WHAT IS CRYPTOCURRENCY?

A cryptocurrency is a virtual or digital currency that is securely encrypted using cryptography and a decentralized online ledger. These currencies operate on a decentralized network and ledger known as blockchain.

Cryptocurrencies enable secure payments through the internet. Transactions are represented through a decentralized ledger containing ledger entries. Crypto translates to the various means by which the virtual currency is encrypted and the techniques used to safeguard each ledger entry. Such techniques could be an elliptical encryption curve, hashing functions, and public/private key pairs.

As of March 2021, there are over 8000 different types of cryptocurrencies. The number keeps growing, with various individuals, businesses, and organizations creating tokens and raising funding through Initial Coin Offerings. The market capitalization of the entire cryptocurrency industry in March 2021 stands at $1.6 trillion. Bitcoin, the first and most prominent coin in the industry, hit a market valuation of $1 trillion after the token attained a market price of $54,000 in February 2021.

Why are Cryptocurrencies Popular?

A primary reason for the hype surrounding cryptocurrencies is the nominal transaction fees charged on the network. Most proponents find the currencies effective to the extent of labeling them "The Future of Money." Besides, cryptocurrencies are not distributed or regulated by a central authority. Therefore, unlike money, the supply of crypto cannot be manipulated by central banks and governments. Most investors find digital currencies as suitable stores of wealth since their value tends to remain stable despite economic or political turmoil in a country.

Here are a couple of reasons why cryptocurrencies are popular.

- **Low Transaction Fees** - Blockchains charge very little transaction fees when processing cryptocurrency transfers. PayPal, for instance, might charge $1.5 for sending over $10, while cryptocurrencies will charge anywhere between $0.1 - $0.5 for the same amount.

- **No Central Authority** - Cryptocurrencies do not have a central governing body. Unlike traditional finance, where central banks control money supply, cryptocurrencies are held within a decentralized ledger. And only through verification of transactions, that more coins are released to the existing supply.

- **Profit Potential** - Cryptocurrencies have high volatility, and their price history suggests that people have been able to generate profits by investing in digital currencies. Most traders buy the coins when the price is low and sell them when the price is high. Investors HODLING on crypto also make profit after saving the digital currencies for a certain time period and cashing out when the price is high.

- **Safe and Private** - No one is actively tracking down your transactions as with traditional finance. Transactions are also cryptographically secured, and transactions are anonymous. Some crypto takes privacy to even a higher level by making it impossible to track down transactions on the blockchain. Such cryptocurrencies are called privacy coins and include Monero, Zcash, and Dash.

- **Increase in Adoption** - In recent years, the adoption rate of digital currencies has grown because of the rise in overall interest, institutional investments, growing network activity of leading coins like Bitcoin, and availability of options like crypto debit cards that help bridge the gap between traditional finance and digital currencies.

Difference between Cryptocurrencies and Traditional Finance

We will establish the primary differences between cryptocurrencies and traditional finance. We are going to look at the distinct features of each technology that distinguishes it from the other.

1. Cryptocurrencies provide anonymity while traditional finance doesn't.

Usually, traditional finance is associated with swiping personal information that's often embedded on credit/debit cards. Payment processors collect this data and may give it to banks, intelligence, unauthorized persons, and governments to track your finances. Anonymity in finance ensures people cannot take advantage of someone's personal information and participate in identity theft or impersonation.

2. Preventing fraud.

No one can counterfeit cryptocurrencies. Besides, it's impossible to arbitrarily reverse a transaction made through digital currency as you would reverse a credit/debit card transaction.

3. Cryptocurrencies have low transactions while traditional payments are expensive.

Digital currencies charge almost zero to minimal transaction fees.

4. No bans.

Traditional finance profiles and accounts are subject to bans and closure. But for crypto wallets, you can access your accounts anywhere and anytime.

5. Open, no barriers to entry.

You only require an internet connection to create and recharge a bitcoin wallet. This means people who previously had no access to a traditional exchange can now indulge in international payments.

6. Cryptocurrencies are decentralized by design, while traditional finance is centralized.

Cryptocurrencies rely on a decentralized network for distribution, transaction, and exchange. Traditional money relies on the backing of governments and central banks to have value. In a decentralized network, all participants are equal and independent.

BENEFITS AND CHALLENGES OF CRYPTOCURRENCIES

2021 saw Bitcoin surge in price and break a psychological resistance at $50,000. Most blockchain experts believe the surge in Bitcoin's price must have been the result of Tesla's CEO Elon Musk, Investing $1.5 Billion in the currency. The rise in interest in the overall crypto industry is leading many investors to weigh their opinion on digital currencies.

To help weigh up the stance on cryptocurrencies, here's a list of their advantages and disadvantages. One thing to note is as with any technology with potential, cryptocurrencies also have disadvantages. However, financial experts have come to acknowledge the benefits of digital currencies and how they will transform the future of money.

Advantages of Cryptocurrencies

1. **Decentralized** - Cryptocurrencies operate on a distributed and decentralized network. No governing bodies or central authorities -but mainly a pool of developers/communities of supporters organizing what direction a particular coin takes. Decentralization ensures digital currencies are free from the manipulation and monopoly of central banks. As a result, this ensures the coin is stable and secure, free from artificial inflation.

2. **Fast and quick** - Cryptocurrencies are a fast, convenient, and reliable means of payment. Transactions take place within seconds. Verification is simple and transactions, domestic as well as cross-border, are processed at a lightning-fast speed. Traditional payment processors such as Mastercard/Visa do provide instant transactions but at the expense of hefty fees. However, for cryptocurrencies, the transactions are within seconds, and the costs are almost negligible.

3. **Wide global acceptance** - Cryptocurrencies are almost becoming the globe's standard currency. They are accepted everywhere, and the adoption rate of virtual currencies is growing with Bitcoin ATMs, crypto payment cards, and crypto payment gateways. In 2019, the number of merchants accepting crypto grew by 600%. The number of cryptocurrency wallets is rising as institutional and retail investors are rising at a rapid scale. Experts believe the coins will also transform how developing nations conduct business as well as help bank millions of unbanked populations.

4. **Privacy and anonymity** - Transactions that take place within the blockchain are completely anonymous and private. Traditional finance transactions are embedded against personal information, while Bitcoin transactions are pegged against a public address. It is only possible to track cryptocurrency transactions to a particular person using sophisticated intelligent cryptography, which is not available to the average person. This means your transactions and information are secure and private. Some coins take this privacy a notch higher by making it impossible even to track transactions through sophisticated cryptography. We earlier mentioned these coins and said they are

called privacy coins. Examples include Monero and Zcash.

5. **Payment Freedom** - Protests in Nigeria helped us see cryptocurrencies' full potential as a tool for liberation. The government banned and placed limits on the finances of right activist groups, making it difficult for these groups to protest against Nigerians' mass killings by police. The groups raised funding from the general public through cryptocurrencies, despite having their traditional bank accounts shut down. Crypto ensures you can pay or be paid anytime, anywhere. There are no limitations, no boundaries, and no central intermediaries to interfere with transactions.

6. **Protecting investors from inflation** - Inflation in Zimbabwe has caused the country's millennial population to resort to cryptocurrencies. Most countries facing inflation are a result of their governments' printing and supplying excess money. For cryptocurrencies, inflation is curbed by having a specified amount of coins being supplied in the market. For example, there will always be 21 million Bitcoins in the world. The scarcity of the coins mean the demand will keep growing, which will therefore increase the price.

Disadvantages of Cryptocurrencies

1. **High volatility** - Cryptocurrencies have high volatility. Price fluctuations are normal and change very fast. Price volatility makes the coins risky for investors, hence keeping away most interested individuals afraid of making losses. Usually, investors require a sound and solid risk management plan to invest in digital assets.

2. **Interference by regulators** - Since several countries do not yet have a legal compliance defined for cryptocurrencies, it results in governmental interference. The governmental involvement unnecessarily hampers innovation around the industry and could lead to the shutdown of potentially revolutionary digital asset products.

3. **Vulnerable to hackers** - Cryptocurrencies are highly secure by design due to their robust encryption protocols. However, cryptocurrencies are traded or stored across exchanges. Cryptocurrency exchanges are not that secure, and hackers have in the past managed to penetrate them —for example, the Bitfinex or Mt Gox hack. While the exchanges have attempted to raise their security standards, the community remains wary of another cyber-attack.

4. **Refunds or Cancellations are impossible** - Cryptocurrencies do not allow one to cancel or automatically refund wrongly sent funds. The only way to ask for a refund is to know the receiver and reason with them to send you back the coins. Otherwise, if the money was sent to the wrong address - it's impossible to recover.

HOW TO USE CRYPTOCURRENCIES?

The best way to spend your cryptocurrencies is first by connecting your crypto wallet with your debit/credit card. In 2021, there are several companies that offer crypto as a payment method to buy their product or services.

Let's consider someone buying a TV set from Amazon. They can pay for the product through a third-party crypto integration platform such as Purse.

Amazon customers using Purse usually select an item they are buying from the Amazon marketplace. They copy this product's URL and paste it into the user interface of Purse. The crypto platform processes the transaction by mostly taking advantage of people who want cryptocurrencies through gift cards. Purse also gives customers a five percent discount on all Amazon products along with an option to negotiate this discount to up to fifteen percent.

There are also other retailers, such as Overstock, which accept bitcoin payments. The retail giant accepts payment through a Coinbase API and allows you to pay from your private wallet. Microsoft also enables consumers to load their accounts with Bitcoin and spend the Xbox and Windows online stores' funds. A trend also began among e-commerce platforms allowing businesses to integrate bitcoin payments on their stores. For example, Shopify gives developers and businesses an option for their customers to pay through crypto.

Payment platforms such as Square, PayPal, and Stripe are also in the process of rolling out crypto features. These will allow users and merchants to send or receive payments in cryptocurrencies.

IS IT SAFE?

The safety of cryptocurrencies was mainly a problem during the early days when the technology was still new. Today, innovators have strong security standards, regulatory requirements, and encryption protocols that ensure the safety of funds. Again, the technology has gained wide acceptance; companies have already put in KYC (Know Your Customer) and AML (Anti Money Laundering) requirements. It is also becoming easier to use cryptocurrencies, and the coins are gaining mainstream adoption from individuals, businesses, and institutional investors.

But are they safe? Are cryptocurrencies a secure means of investment or payment?

Nowadays, cryptocurrencies are not as susceptible to hacks as they were during the initial years. Nevertheless, there are three major risks associated with digital coins. These risks include:

1. The possibility of losing a private key and subsequently losing access to your crypto.
2. An unauthorized person having access to your private key and subsequently stealing your crypto.
3. Coins losing value due to high volatility.

Let's analyze the risk factors one at a time starting with crypto losing value due to volatility. Like all assets, even in traditional finance, loss of value is a common risk. All investments could lose or gain value; all you need to curb losses are good risk management mechanisms.

Losing the private key is one of the most common risks with cryptocurrencies. A private key gives you ownership of your coins. It means with the private key; you can access, spend, or transfer your Bitcoins or any other tokens. If the private key falls into the hands of an unauthorized person, your tokens become vulnerable resulting in the loss or theft of your coins. The loss of private keys subsequently results in the loss of access to cryptocurrencies. Securing and protecting the private keys facilitate the safety of investments or crypto funds. It is synchronized to protecting passwords and personal identification information. Generally, cryptocurrencies are safe and a suitable way for keeping your financial investments safe.

2

HOW CRYPTOCURRENCY WORKS?

GETTING TO KNOW THE LEDGER

B eginners may find it hard to differentiate between cryptocurrencies and blockchain technology. Simply put, blockchain technology is the underlying framework upon which cryptocurrencies are held. People also need to understand there are far more practical applications of the blockchain apart from digital currencies.

As an emerging technology much like big data, machine learning and artificial intelligence - businesses around the world are tinkering with innovative ways of implementing the blockchain beyond finance. Hundreds of thousands of innovations have sprung out across the world and ignited a revolution in dozens of industries such as transportation, data merging, data consolidation and authentication, supply chains and logistics, streaming and copyright ownership for artists, eCommerce, medical informatics, and human resource.

In this chapter, we are going to discuss *"How Cryptocurrency Works"* and the following section gives you details about the inner workings of the distributed ledger. You will differentiate between blockchain and traditional banking. Finally, you are going to understand how blockchains work, how cryptocurrency transactions are verified, how cryptocurrencies are created as well as consensus mechanisms for validating the ledger.

Blockchain is mostly defined as a distributed ledger. A distributed ledger is more like a public database but with several attributes such as immutability, anonymity, and encryption. We are going to discuss these features in detail later. However, it's important to see the distributed ledger as a database whose data sets are spread across an entire network. The encryption and immutability of the network make it impossible for network participants to alter any data sets.

A distributed ledger can be spread across the world and is availed to everyone that can access an internet connection. At the core, any network participant can run the ledger by adding data and cross-examining the network. However, once a piece of data has been added to the ledger, it cannot be removed nor altered. The ledger is stratified in layers called blocks. Hence the name blockchain, "a chain of blocks.' A block is simply a stack, list, or set of data. Several blocks form a chain. The immutability concept states that data within a blockchain cannot be changed. This makes blockchain an effective medium of data storage for future use. Again, anyone on the network can see what's happening on the network, which to some extent could come in handy when democratizing organizational activities.

A new block is added to the chain after a particular duration. This duration is referred to as block time and for example on the Bitcoin blockchain, the average block time is 10 minutes. This means a block is created after every ten minutes on the blockchain network. The block contains a list of verified transactions, upon whose verification a block reward (composed of bitcoins) is released to the network and awarded to the winning miner. A miner is a participant on the blockchain who ensures transactions are validated by contributing computing power. The network often rewards the winning miner with a number of cryptocurrencies after the validation of each successive block. And this is how cryptocurrencies (in the case of bitcoins) are injected into circulation.

Distributed ledgers differ from traditional ledgers in the sense that participants do not have to trust each other. The blockchain automates trust on the network through consensus mechanisms. Consensus allows distributed components of a system to come into an agreement without the need for a central authority. On the other hand, traditional ledgers rely on a central authority to validate and deploy trust across the network. However, decentralized/distributed ledgers are costly to secure, maintain, and run. Traditional ledgers are risky because security is dependent on the ability of a central authority to wade off vulnerability. For example, a dissatisfied employee could delete a database since a traditional ledger is not immutable. Cybercriminals could hack into the central authority. Placing both personal data and information of network participants at risk. For the decentralized ledger, each network participant maintains an equal version of the database. To modify or update the blockchain, the ledger sends out a proposal to all participants (or nodes) and the ability to modify the blockchain is dependent on consensus. Until a number of these nodes approve the proposal, will a valid transaction/modification take place on the network?

CRYPTOCURRENCY TRANSACTIONS

Cryptocurrencies are used to deploy storage and security of finances. A distributed ledger at the core is a record of all cryptocurrency transactions taking place within the blockchain. Verification of cryptocurrency transactions utilizes computing power, which helps miners to solve complex mathematical equations. Solving these equations generates more coins into the network, and verifies transactions. The individuals solving these equations are called miners and they are rewarded with a particular number of digital currencies. They in turn exchange these coins for fiat through cryptocurrency exchanges. Miners can also trade their rewarded coins for other cryptocurrencies on the exchanges or store them for future use on cryptocurrency wallets.

The hype around cryptocurrencies in the investment world lies profoundly in their high volatility. Digital currencies can fluctuate in value within small durations. This makes them risky but highly profitable. As a result, individuals have found a source of income from trading such digital coins and selling them when the value is high. A phenomenon that has created overnight millionaires.

Most of the skepticism surrounding cryptocurrencies arises from regulation. The digital currency world is a nascent technology and has gone unregulated in most parts of the world. This has created a loophole for criminals to take advantage of and scam investors' money in the name of crypto. Besides, cryptocurrencies are usually anonymous and transactions take place through complicated addresses that are impossible to associate with a face. This has influenced the financing of illegal activities such as the purchase and trading of illegal stuff on the dark web. Black market e-commerce has thrived as a result of the privacy features of digital coins such as the silk road marketplace scandal.

While the privacy feature has been used by criminals, it has also been used for good. Protest organizations in Nigeria raised charity funding through Bitcoin to finance their activist operations. This followed after the government censored and banned financial accounts linked to the human rights organizations following the #ENDSARS movement in 2021.

This shows how Bitcoin and other cryptocurrencies can also function as a liberal tool in a highly undemocratic society.

Basics of Cryptocurrency Transaction

This is how basic cryptocurrency transactions take place.

A user creates a profile on a digital currency exchange like Coinbase or Binance. On the exchange, the user uses a credit/debit card or any other payment plan to purchase cryptocurrencies. Once purchased, the user creates a digital wallet for storing the coins. The wallet containing the coins is linked to a public address. This is the public address that one sees and uses when they want to send cryptocurrencies to your wallet. Remember it's impossible to recover coins sent to the wrong address.

Usually, when a cryptocurrencies transaction takes place, the public address is recorded on the decentralized ledger. The ledger records the receiving user's public address as the transaction output and the sender's public address as the transaction input.

All aspects of the digital coin system are designed to ensure transactions are implemented, created, and verified within the network. The system also ensures that all of these transactions are recorded on a decentralized ledger that is accessible by anyone on the blockchain. We can also view transactions as data structures that encode value and transfer this value across participants of a network. Ideally, each piece of transaction is entered into a ledger as a single entry.

This single entry contains any number of signatures above two authorizing and validating that the funds in question can be spent. Finally, the cryptocurrency system broadcasts this entry (s) across the entire network and each network participant verifies this transaction and passes it to the next participant. The last bit is having the transaction or entry as part of more entries on the network, which are included within one block. Once an entire block has been confirmed, usually depending on the block time of a particular blockchain, the funds being transacted change ownership, and the cycle repeats.

Cryptocurrency transactions involve transaction fees. These fees are meant to compensate miners within the network and to also facilitate network operation. Miners collect these fees as rewards for validating transaction blocks. Typically, cryptocurrency wallets will compute transaction fees automatically. The amount of transaction fees depends on the size of the transaction, and the size of a transaction is usually measured in kilobytes (KBs). Additionally, note that the overall transaction fees fluctuate on Ethereum and Bitcoin's network as a result of market forces.

Also, note that cryptocurrency transaction fees influence the priority of processing a transaction. For example, a transaction with sufficient fees will likely be processed quickly. While the latter will be included in a subsequent block and get delayed. By design, transaction fees are not a must for a transaction to take place. However, a transaction without fees will take forever to process. One that has plenty of fees will be processed quickly.

CRYPTOGRAPHY AND SECURITY

In the vast sea of finances and technology, security is the single most important aspect of any institution offering

HOW CRYPTOCURRENCY WORKS? | 43

fintech services. The security of centralized payment networks such as banks depends on a central authority that controls, verifies, and vets users. A decentralized system on the other hand depends on its participants to maintain and uphold its security. How is this made possible? Especially in a world full of mistrust, cybercriminals, and spammers.

The Bitcoin network for example gives participants the responsibility of securing the blockchain based on a model known as proof of work. The main goal of the proof of work algorithm is ensuring no extra coins are created on a network. It holds that a community of miners must earn the coins generated by the system by validating transactions. Furthermore, the concept solves the problem of double-spending. That is spending the coins more than once, and therefore making the coins worthless. Proof of Work and Proof of Stake algorithms provide the network with a level of complexity which makes it hard to acquire cryptocurrencies. This gives value to the coins, as the complexity level of solving the equation rises.

Traditional payment systems ensure the security of fiat by hiding user identification details such as credit card numbers. The security of the network is then boosted through end-to-end encryption to ensure an initial charge isn't repeated over and over again by unscrupulous persons. Secure end-to-end encryption also protects accounts from eavesdroppers and interference by third parties who could interfere with the network. Again, traditional banks have a role in protecting customer data to prevent incidents of identity theft, impersonation, and fraudulent sale of personal information.

The best thing about cryptography is that transactions are tied to a particular value and recipient. Users do not reveal any financial information that would aid in identity theft. Transactions are linked to public addresses. Each wallet or crypto storage is accessed privately by a user through a private key. Transactions on the Bitcoin network are immutable and therefore protected from modification. This makes the blockchain bulletproof and impossible to suffer from eavesdropping. This makes it prudent to even broadcast cryptocurrency transactions through insecure public networks such as Bluetooth or WIFI without exposing the network to security risks.

By design, Satoshi Nakamoto invented the Proof of Work mechanism to increase security with the increase in computation power. This concept loosely translates that the more computational power and resources fed into the network will subject a hacker to have more of that amount, to successfully penetrate the network. Each network participant (or node) contributes computational power and this gives each user the responsibility to maintain the security of the platform. While this is a lot of power to leave in the hands of users, one would wonder whether the users cannot corroborate against bringing down the blockchain. This is impossible since the proof of work algorithm creates a competition among the nodes to win the block reward. So, each node is trying to bring in as much power as possible to solve the algorithm before everyone else.

STANCE OF CRYPTOCURRENCIES ACROSS THE WORLD

The rise of cryptocurrencies and decentralized finance has attracted both hate and love from governments around the world. There are those progressive governments who view cryptocurrencies as a means to bridge financial literacy across populations. Those daring enough to welcome the idea of liberated finance away from central banks and traditional institutions. Governments whose regulatory framework and taxation remain in favor of crypto. Some governments are even considering building their stablecoins, while there are those like China, which already banned digital currencies but are still building their digital stable coin. Others like Nigeria have a tough stance against crypto and view it as a threat to national security.

Let's look at the perspective of 4 different countries across the world and their stance on digital currencies.

United States

The regulation and taxation of cryptocurrencies in the United States depend on state laws. Different state jurisdictions have different definitions of digital currencies. However, the US Financial Crimes Enforcement Network does not define cryptocurrency as legal tender. Exchanges are also viewed differently depending on different state policies.

The main regulatory body in the US, the Securities and Exchange Commission announced it was going to apply security laws on exchanges, cryptocurrencies, and all digital asset companies. There is also Christopher Giancarlo, the commissioner at the Commodities Futures Trading Commission who holds that bitcoin and other cryptocurrencies are commodities. Giancarlo has earned a reputation as a crypto-friendly regulator and won the affection of the bitcoin community.

India

India already outlawed bitcoin and other cryptocurrencies. While the central bank of India has already issued several warnings to crypto participants; the regulation does not censor cryptocurrency exchanges. The government believes digital currencies are a threat to both political and economic dynamics. Especially when used to fund illegal activities or finance terrorism. The government of India has already formed a body to oversee and ensure the elimination of all cryptocurrency activities.

Switzerland

Switzerland has been described as one of the most crypto-friendly environments in the world. This is why Facebook registered the Libra Association in Geneva. Zurich's town of Zug has earned the reputation of holding so many crypto events and projects that it has been nicknamed crypto valley. The town is home to Cardano Foundation and the Ethereum Foundation. However, the country requires Cryptocurrency exchanges to be registered with the Financial Market Supervisory Authority.

Singapore

While Singapore doesn't view cryptocurrencies as legal tender, the country has emerged as a more crypto-friendly environment for ICOs and digital asset trading. However, the state urges its people to be cautious about crypto and understand the risks of volatility before dipping their toes in. Singapore has held 15 of the largest initial coin offerings.

3

LEARNING THE DIFFERENT CURRENCIES

Before reading this section, it's worth noting how impossible it is to discuss the entire list of cryptocurrencies. Owing to a statistic released this year by CoinmarketCap indicating there are over 9,000 cryptocurrencies in the world today. The majority of them enjoy backing, investment support, and development support from a substantial population of the fintech community. Bitcoin was only a trendsetter that sparked a wave of thousands of cryptocurrency projects. The coin has also been forked to create hard fork coins such as Bitcoin Cash, Bitcoin Gold, while other developers across the world have launched big projects such as Vitallik Buterin's Ethereum. There is Cardano, Chainlink, XRP, Monero, Zcash, Dash, Litecoin and so many more.

The role of this entire legion of crypto spinoffs aims at leveraging decentralized finance, blockchain technology, and digital finance across diverse industries in energy, health, privacy, machine learning, artificial intelligence, data science and big data, supply chain management and logistics, content creation, ownership and distribution, security, democracy, and finance.

In the section that follows we are going to discuss why there are so many cryptocurrencies in the world and what inspired their creation.

WHY ARE THERE SO MANY CRYPTOCURRENCIES?

Decentralization belongs to no one and is controlled by everyone. This means anyone with the technical and financial capacity to create a cryptocurrency, can do so. Besides, blockchains have emerged that allow developers to build and deploy their cryptocurrencies on top of other cryptocurrencies. A good example is Ethereum and its Ethereum Virtual Machine. Such cryptocurrencies have a utility function and operate on an already developed blockchain infrastructure. Furthermore, there are app/platform cryptocurrencies that are built on top of utility cryptocurrencies. An example of this is the Augur cryptocurrency, which was built and launched on the Ethereum network.

When Satoshi Nakamoto created Bitcoin, developers noted a huge potential for the creation of more and better cryptocurrencies using his technology. Most of these developers wanted to create a better version of the blockchain and a better version of cryptocurrencies. For example, an ex-Google Engineer Charlie Lee pondered the idea of creating a lightweight version of bitcoin. Like what silver is, to gold. The result of his innovation was Litecoin, which was faster, cheaper to transact, and easier to mine than Bitcoin. Other developers and entrepreneurs followed suit and ended up creating plenty of altcoins.

Reasons for the Existence of so Many Cryptocurrencies

1. **High investment returns** - the cryptocurrency boom has been associated with the massive success of Bitcoin. Some traders and investors have turned into overnight millionaires. When the coin first appeared, not so many people showed interest. And the little that did, didn't care enough. Approaching 2017 and as the value continued soaring from $100 to the 2017 bull run, the world took note of the

coin. Other altcoins boomed as well following Bitcoin's $20,000 record price.

2. **Media headlines and press releases** - the buzz created after the success of Bitcoin created a legion of web writers, journalists, and analysts who were inspired to write about digital currencies. This created more interest across diverse sectors as most businesses, innovators, and governments sort blockchain to solve problems across multiple industries.

3. **Forks** - A few cryptocurrencies have risen through forking. For example, Bitcoin Cash, Litecoin, and Bitcoin Gold are attributed to forking on the Bitcoin network. While Ethereum Classic and Litecoin Cash are attributed to Litecoin.

4. **Research, scientific innovation, and progressive development** - The need for progress and development across the economy and technology sectors has created the urge to tinker with innovations. So many projects have given birth to cryptocurrencies and the competition is still ongoing. Each project aims to win the love of the cryptocurrency community and therefore brings with it many innovative features, solutions, and efficiency to the blockchain community.

5. **ICO Boom** - Initial Coin Offerings boomed

between 2015 - 2017. Projects were raising millions of dollars from these events. The promise of capital to fund innovations catalyzed more developers to innovate and create, which spurred a plethora of cryptocurrencies.

The cryptocurrency field is expanding. More projects are being launched every month and the global community is preparing for the next big digital asset. The nascence of the industry has led to governments employing research to find out better regulator frameworks and taxation methods. In the meantime, proponents hope digital currencies will go mainstream and will one day become a major payment method.

HOW ARE CRYPTOCURRENCIES CREATED?

The most challenging thing about cryptocurrencies is not in their creation but their adoption. Anyone with programming knowledge can easily create a crypto coin. As a matter of fact, one can build upon existing code that is easily available as open-source on platforms such as Github. A programmer could also pick an open-source project, choose the algorithm they wish to implement, and conduct a fork. For entrepreneurs and businesspeople without knowledge of coding, they could use altcoin development services such as CryptoNote and SHA-256. Such services charge a fee to create, host, and maintain cryptocurrencies.

In their most basic form, cryptocurrencies come to existence once transactions are confirmed. These transactions are confirmed through a process known as mining. However, not all coins are generated through mining.

What is Mining?

Mining involves a distributed team of individuals taking part in solving a cryptographic equation by contributing computing resources to validate blocks of data/transactions and adding those blocks into a decentralized ledger. The individuals taking part are rewarded with cryptocurrencies and this is how coins are injected into the circulation.

But let's look at cryptocurrency mining using Bitcoin as our case study. Bitcoin mining breeds two benefits to the network. One - addition of more Bitcoins into the economy. Two-securing the network and making the blockchain more trustworthy. A typical Bitcoin miner clumps blocks of transactions together and records them on a public ledger/blockchain. Computer nodes across the network then take part in managing and maintenance of these records for future validation.

The Bitcoin miner adds a block of transactions into the network and the entire network participants ensure those transactions are accurate. Furthermore, miners ensure that a single transaction does not get duplicated as a result of double-spending. Unlike fiat currencies, digital currencies are somewhat easy to reproduce and the work of the miners is to prevent such incidences.

THE MOST COMMON CRYPTOCURRENCIES

Besides Bitcoin, we are going to look at some of the most popular cryptocurrencies. This is because we cannot promise to outline and describe all the digital assets in existence today. A huge chunk of factors influences the ranking of cryptocurrencies. I did put much thought into the considerations to create a comprehensive list of the ten most important digital assets.

Ethereum (ETH)

Ether is the native token of the Ethereum network. It's a most sought-after cryptocurrency among decentralized finance developers who want to deploy their projects using Ethereum's smart contracts. According to ranking by Coinmarketcap, Ethereum is the 2nd largest cryptocurrency by market capitalization. The coin's founder is Vitallik Buterik and it was launched in 2015.

Litecoin (LTC)

Litecoin emerged only a while after the birth of Bitcoin in 2011. The coin was created by a former Google engineer, Charlie Lee. Litecoin's main aim was to offer a lightweight alternative for Bitcoin. Lee's vision was a coin that would be easier to mine, cheaper to transact, and quicker than bitcoin. Today, Litecoin commands a market capitalization of $10.1 billion and is trading at $200.

Cardano (ADA)

Computer engineers, cryptographers, mathematicians, and innovative researchers came together to build the Cardano blockchain using a research-based approach. One of the founders of Cardano was among Ethereum's initial founders and disagreed with Ethereum's development team on the direction of the coin. As a result, Charles Hoskinson left and went on to create Cardano. The research-based approach employed by Hoskinson and other team members was based on the premise of peer-reviewed studies and extensive experimentation. It's therefore not by chance that the team behind the project has written almost 100 scholarly papers on blockchain technology.

Bitcoin Cash

Disagreements among Bitcoin developers caused a divide that created two camps across the community. The issue was scalability and how the Bitcoin blockchain was going to adapt in the future, in the wake of massive traffic. Today, Bitcoin cash has grown into a largely accepted cryptocurrency that commands a lot of support and respect from prominent figures such as Roger Ver and MarcdeMesel. Various utility platforms have risen on the Bitcoin Cash blockchain such as Noise.cash and Read.cash. Presently, BHC has a market capitalization of $9 billion and is trading at $600.

Polkadot

The creators of Polkadot had a vision of making it possible for blockchains to become interoperable. By design, the blockchain is meant to connect one blockchain to another - whether permissioned or permissionless. The protocols also make it possible for oracles of data to link and work together systematically. Polkadot is a promising project. Its creator Gavin Wood was one of the 5 co-founders of the Ethereum network. Today, DOT commands a huge market capitalization of $11.8 billion and is trading at $20.

Chainlink

Chainlink bridges the gap between blockchains and data. Through smart contracts, Chainlink ensures blockchains can implement external data in an open and trusted way. The blockchain utilizes smart contracts to communicate with outside databases. Chainlink's creators are Steve Ellis and Sergey Nazarov. Presently, the market capitalization of Chainlink is $9.1 billion and the price for a piece of LINK is $29.

Binance Coin

Binance Coin is a native utility coin of the Binance Smart Chain, developed by leading cryptocurrency exchange Binance. Initially, the coin was built on top of Ethereum as an ERC-20 token before launching its own mainnet. As of today, Binance commands a market capitalization of $7 billion and goes for $200.

Monero (XMR)

Monero falls under the category of privacy coins. Privacy coins are securely encrypted from tracing and are completely private. The blockchain is also open source and came to existence in 2014. It's worth noting the development of this cryptocurrency is funded through donations. And the development is led by a community of cryptography enthusiasts. The main focus of the coin is to push decentralization and scalability to another level.

Tether (USDT)

Tether is a stablecoin. Stablecoins are usually digital currencies whose value is tethered to a fiat currency in order to curb volatility. The price of tether is tied to the US dollar and allows users to easily compute and transfer cryptocurrencies to US dollars in an efficient way. Stablecoins were built to encourage more people to get into cryptocurrencies and to make the process of exchanging fiat-crypto easy.

Stellar (XML)

Stellar is an enterprise-based blockchain solution for financial platforms to deploy large transactions. This makes it painless, fast, and easy for banks and investment companies to process large transactions that would otherwise take days. The blockchain saves institutions a large amount of costs and the transactions are conducted almost instantaneously. Stellar's creator is among the founding members of Ripple (XRP), another digital currency. Presently, Stellar commands a market capitalization of $6.5 billion, and each piece costs $0.45.

WHAT ARE ALTCOINS?

Alt stands for alternative. Altcoins fully translate to alternatives of Bitcoin.

Other than Bitcoin, there are over 9,000 other cryptocurrencies called altcoins. Ideally, the price of altcoins is by design meant to perform in sync with Bitcoin.

However, most of these coins differ from Bitcoin either by their consensus mechanism or their ability to implement smart contract futures. Similarities between Bitcoin and altcoins lie in their ability to process large data sets and huge transactions; particularly, they are similar in code and employ an underlying peer-to-peer mechanism to process blocks of data. Also, some altcoins came into existence as a solution to some of Bitcoin's woeful problems such as high transaction fees, scalability issues, and mining challenges posed by the Proof of Work algorithm.

For instance, the Proof of Stake consensus mechanism is an altcoin modification of the Proof of Work algorithm. PoW is time-consuming and energy-intensive. By improving upon the limitations of Bitcoin, altcoins aspire to become the next big coin.

TYPES OF ALTCOINS

Mining-based altcoins - Such altcoins are generated through mining. There are those altcoins that are mined using the Proof of Work method or Proof of Stake method. Both methods involve solving a computation equation in order to validate a block. Mine-based altcoins include Monero, Zcash, and Litecoin.

- **Pre-mined coins** - These are coins with a fixed

supply and that are already distributed to the economy before being listed on an exchange. A good example is Ripple (XRP).

- **Stablecoins** - Stablecoins were invented to solve the inherent problem of volatility across crypto markets. They were meant to provide a non-fluctuating digital currency for individual daily transactions. These coins are tied to the value of a commodity, precious metal, or fiat currency such as the US dollar.

- **Security Tokens** - Share some underlying similarities with traditional stock, especially by providing the promise of equity or payouts in the form of dividends. Usually, investors acquire security tokens through Initial Coin Offerings.

- **Utility Tokens** - Utility tokens support the functionality of a network in a decentralized environment. They are used to purchase gifts, redeem rewards, or purchase services. A good example of a utility token is Filecoin, which enables users to buy storage space on their blockchain.

CHOOSING YOUR CURRENCY

Take the following steps when choosing a cryptocurrency to invest in.

Research on your own

Arm yourself with enough information. Do not just read press releases and marketing information. Pay attention to the historical analysis of a given coin. Observe the trends and be a better judge. Identify points that indicate the potential for growth and the potential for returns. Read through the whitepapers of given cryptocurrencies and understand the utility of a given coin. What problem is it solving and does it have the potential for mass adoption?

Choose your Risk

Cryptocurrencies are profitable mainly because they have a high-risk level. This risk level is associated with the digital currency market's high volatility. There are so many cryptocurrencies out there and you have to invest only what you can afford to lose. Customize your own risk management method perhaps with the help of fintech analysts. You might consider spreading your risks across different coins to mitigate losses when one coin suffers heavy downsides.

Remain informed about Initial Coin Offerings

Look out for Initial Coin Offerings. But you should research the team behind a given ICO and ponder on your own how beneficial the project is. Essentially, do you think the project has potential for adoption and does it guarantee a return on your investment?

Be patient and avoid FOMO (Fear of Missing Out)

Monitor the market closely and avoid rushing to investment and making emotional decisions. Take your time to observe market trends, put your independent research in mind and make informed decisions. This will put you in good shape before investing in any cryptocurrency.

II

BUT BEFORE YOU TRADE

4

REGULATIONS, TAXES, AND SCAMS

In this chapter, we are going to discuss the regulatory environment for cryptocurrencies. How different governments, central banks, and authorities view crypto and how favorable or unfavorable it is to take part in the industry.

CRYPTOCURRENCY REGULATIONS DIFFER IN COUNTRIES

Cryptocurrencies crossed into the regulator's footlight back in 2017 following the bitcoin bull run. Policymakers sparked conversations regarding the regulation of digital currencies. A few governments who saw bitcoin banned it within their boundaries. Other governments with a more progressive stand for emerging technologies sort to create laws that would make it favorable to trade crypto. However, there was a looming gap between the intersection of cryptocurrency, finance, and regulations. From the very beginning, people saw cryptocurrencies as a liberal tool to liberate individuals and businesses from the financial monopoly of central banks. Apparently, it became more prudent for cryptocurrency proponents to work alongside the very regulators (central banks and governments) they wished to disrupt. A fundamental problem from these early days remained the lack of regulatory guidance or framework to follow in the digital asset class industry. And this has remained a problem to this day as authorities and associated stakeholders research, experiment, and tinker with innovative methods to regulate, tax, and ward off scams in the cryptocurrency industry.

The cryptocurrency market is on a growing trend. Different innovations are sprouting up and as it has emerged, developers are yet to realize the full capabilities of the blockchain. First of all, there is no standard regulation practice overseeing the use and trade of cryptocurrencies. Second, the regulations are different and vary from country to country and finally, there are those countries that haven't announced their legal perspective of Bitcoin and digital currencies. All of these countries are home to millions of cryptocurrency traders, innovations, businesses, and enterprises; but the rules are different. A good approach to playing according to the rules is conducting independent research. This research should aim at establishing the regulatory environment within one's jurisdiction, country, or state. Breaking down the policies of your country and updating yourself with proper guidance are key considerations when dipping your toes into the complicated phenomenon that is cryptocurrency.

Above I mentioned that some governments are yet to announce their legal position on digital currencies. But a common practice among all governments is the issuance of warnings and notices cautioning people to beware of the pitfalls of crypto investment. Most of these warnings are from central banks and are in part, designed to sensitize the general public on the basic differences between fiat and crypto. These notices inform people about the inherent volatility of cryptocurrencies and warn them of the possibility of losses. In fact, the notices caution citizens that the government would not provide any legal recourse in case of loss when investing in digital currencies. While such information is important for sensitization against scams, I don't think it's favorable for catalyzing the growth of emergent technology. This is because it could create fear.

For example, the government of Pakistan through its Central Bank issued a warning to the public about the potential of cryptocurrencies to support and finance illegal activities such as terrorism and money laundering. More governments took such steps in illegalizing cryptocurrencies and banning all activities that involved the use of digital coins. These governments include Algeria, Nepal, Vietnam, Morocco, Bolivia, Nigeria, and many more. Some jurisdictions such as Canada, the Isle of Man, and Australia have expanded regulatory frameworks around counterterrorism, money laundering, crime syndicates, and drug dealings to include the use of cryptocurrencies. Other jurisdictions such as China, Lithuania, Iran, Bangladesh, Colombia, and Lesotho have imposed indirect restrictions that limit the processing of crypto-based transactions. For example, China already banned all crypto exchange activities in the country.

Some countries still see cryptocurrency as a threat but instead chose to regulate operations. A good example is the United States, the Netherlands, and New Zealand. Nonetheless, not all countries in the world view digital currencies as a threat. Some such as Switzerland, Seychelles, Cayman Islands, Spain, Belarus, Malta, and Luxembourg view cryptocurrency as a means to attract investment into their countries. Switzerland for example is said to be one of the most crypto-friendly countries in the world. These countries have the perspective that the underlying technology behind cryptocurrencies is fundamental for progress.

A country like Venezuela has even gone a step further to develop its own cryptocurrency and digital payment system. While some countries such as the United Kingdom view the cryptocurrency industry as too small to warrant bans, regulations, or sanctions.

Also, while researching the regulatory environment of digital asset classes, it's worth establishing taxation rules. Taxation has been a challenge for governments, but most of them have already cracked the code. However, different countries have different categorizations of cryptocurrencies for the main purpose of taxation. For instance, Israel taxes crypto as an asset class, Switzerland classifies them as foreign currency while Spain and Argentina subject them to income tax.

REGULATIONS YOU NEED TO BE AWARE OF

According to a 2019 report by the Financial Stability Board (FSB), there are three concerns associated with the jurisdictional regulations around cryptocurrencies. These are:

1. Regulatory gaps more particularly when an asset remains outside the purview of a given market's regulator and oversight.

2. Whether the existing cryptocurrencies were created to function outside existing regulations.
3. Absence of a global standard of regulation.

The regulation of the corporate bond market, stocks, treasury bonds, foreign exchanges, and derivatives can be taken into consideration when drafting policies around digital currencies. However, stakeholders need to coordinate policymaking with other financial authorities and factor in challenges such as consumer protection, concerns posed by money laundering, cybersecurity, trust and transparency, custody and settlement, as well as system integrity. In the Financial Stability Board's report, policymakers such as the Basel Committee drafted regulation of cryptocurrencies based on three significant groupings:

1. Quantification of the potential of both direct and indirect exposure of banks to crypto assets.
2. Clarification of the rationality of the bank's exposure to crypto-assets.
3. Close monitoring and observation of fintech developments related to crypto-assets and evaluating the implications of these developments across traditional banking sectors.

One of the most plausible developments is the connection between cryptocurrencies and money laundering. According to the UK's Financial Conduct Authority (or FCA), banking firms ought to scrutinize a client deriving business from them using revenue from cryptocurrency activities. In a letter dubbed, **Dear CEO**, the evaluations should take place in either of the following instances:

1. If the business provides services to crypto-asset exchanges with the implication of conversion fluctuations between fiat-crypto or vice versa.
2. If the parties in question generate their income from crypto-related trading activities.
3. If the firm in question is planning to organize, engage, or advise on an Initial Coin Offerings.

Notwithstanding some regulators have also taken upon them the role of regulating cryptocurrencies in the same as securities. Why so?

According to the US Securities and Exchange Commission, a security is a 'share' indicative of an investor's participation or interest in a particular company, enterprise, business, or profit-making corporation. The evidence of participation is in the form of a certificate, instrument, contract - which could be either in written-printed form or electronic. Securities could take any of the following forms:

1. Shares of bonds, stocks, debentures, asset-backed securities, and notes proving indebtedness.
2. Investment contracts, certificate of deposit in the event of future subscription, profit-sharing agreement certificate.
3. Derivatives such as warrants and options.
4. Fractional undivided interests in mineral rights (oil, gas, etc.).
5. Certificate of participation, voting trust, trust certificates, certificate of assignments.
6. Proprietary or nonproprietary certificates of membership.
7. Any other instrument that the commission might determine as security in the future.

SEC chairman Jay Clayton insists that while instruments such as Initial Coin Offerings are effective ways for entrepreneurs to raise financing; they require essential disclosures for investor protection and must abide by security laws. He insists that slight deviations from the basic structure of securities such as in the case of digital currencies; doesn't mean an instrument has to deviate from laws governing securities. In a notice published on the SEC website, Clayton finds no reason to not refer to cryptocurrencies as securities. He poses the question of what difference in form does a traditional stock recorded in a central ledger have, compared to an enterprise-based interest recorded on a decentralized ledger. Both interests might differ in the way transactions are conducted, but that doesn't change the fundamental nature of the interest.

MEET THE BROKER

A cryptocurrency broker facilitates the buying and selling of cryptocurrencies by acting as an intermediary. While brokers set their customized market prices, cryptocurrency exchanges also facilitate buying and selling of coins; but they charge trading fees. One can start trading cryptocurrencies either through a broker or an exchange.

Brokers usually locate sellers and buyers of cryptocurrencies. They identify those buyers and sellers with large amounts of cryptocurrencies and pull them together. Normally, the settlement process provided by a broker is more convenient compared to an exchange. This makes trading flexible, faster, and reliable.

Here are the questions you should ask about a broker before choosing one. These questions will help inform your decision and help you choose the most appropriate cryptocurrency broker.

1. **Does the broker hedge?** - It's important for

traders to hedge their positions to mitigate losses. This provides clarity on the type of risk management approach that a broker has employed. Failure to hedge cryptocurrencies might cause lots of losses due to high volatility.

2. **Does the broker trade over the weekend?** - Unlike the stock market which closes during weekends, crypto markets operate 7 days a week on a 24/7 basis. Some brokers might not trade during the weekends, while others might trade. Take this factor as one of your considerations while choosing a crypto broker.

3. **What are the costs?** - Establish the amount of commissions charged by your intended brokers. Besides, all brokers will also offer margin accounts. Factor all this into consideration and determine what your profit margin could be.

4. **Is the broker offering short sales** - Most brokers restrict their cryptocurrency products to long sales as a result of having access to few hedging solutions. Find out whether a broker provides short sales. Shorting protects traders from making losses during downsides.

THE RULE OF THE BROKER

Legitimate brokers are licensed, authorized to operate, and regulated. You pose huge risks to your investment capital when you choose an unregulated cryptocurrency broker. Two things could happen, they could disappear with your funds and you will not be able to do anything about it. And two, they could sell your personal information. Do a background check before choosing any cryptocurrency broker. Ensure the broker has an active license.

Most regulators demand that cryptocurrency brokers inform customers about the risks associated with cryptocurrencies. For example, The European Union dictates a broker should notify the client that crypto trading is an unregulated venture in the EU. This warning must also inform the customer about the complexity of digital currencies and the high risk of loss.

Additionally, brokers are expected to indicate the ease of price fluctuations across cryptocurrency markets. High volatility translates to high risks and a high potential for returns at the same time. A broker is supposed to suggest all events and inform the client of the possible losses and returns. Again, investors without a solid risk management plan should not trade in virtual assets. First, an investor will need to acquaint themselves with the required knowledge in specific virtual assets. And then, they should conduct a fundamental analysis of any product and understand the features and risks associated with different products.

Digital asset brokers should take their legal obligations in high regard. Mainly because prospects are certainly going to use these regulations as benchmarks to gauge the legitimacy of a broker. No one wants to invest with a suspicious broker that has already failed to file its taxes. Close attention to how a broker conducts himself might reveal potential greenlights for a good relationship with them; or red flags that urge you to stay away. A professional broker acts fairly, professionally, and honestly. Such brokers put the interest of a client first, and will never provide misleading information.

KNOW YOUR TAXES

Regulatory authorities seem to agree about one thing when it comes to cryptocurrencies. That they should be taxed. Interestingly, it turns out they can't agree whether they should be taxed as currencies or commodities.

United States tax agency, the Internal Revenue Services (IRS) defined virtual currencies as property. This definition came into work back in 2014. As property, the IRS outlines virtual currencies are liable to taxation from the capital gains. It doesn't matter whether these gains are short-term or long-term. The tax is imposed depending on the amount of time one has held on to a virtual asset. Just like it is with taxable property.

The IRS made it a requirement for citizens in the US to disclose all taxable transactions associated with cryptocurrencies. Such transactions would take the form of:

- Receiving forked/mined cryptocurrencies
- Exchanging virtual currencies for fiat - also known as cashing out of a wallet
- Using cryptocurrencies to make payments for goods or services
- Exchanging crypto to crypto.

Nevertheless, note that taxation regulations vary from country to country. But in light of this, all regulatory frameworks might have the following benchmarks in common:

1. When cashing out, authorities will evaluate the basis price of the crypto in question. For instance, one would be required to pay tax on the short-term capital gain if they bought a virtual asset at $1000 and sold it three months later at $5000. This tax is imposed in the form of income tax. However, when selling crypto that's been acquired through mining,

the profit made from here is taxed as business income. Since this is similar to taxing work done. And it also helps individuals deduct the expenses associated with mining.

2. Exchange virtual currencies - When you exchange let's say Bitcoin for Litecoin, you are selling Bitcoin. This means you should report any price differences between the price you bought Bitcoin and the price you are selling. Most major exchanges provide cutting-edge solutions for helping users report taxes and lessen the burden of determining price fluctuations.

3. Purchases - Taxation on personal purchases is also factored in when buying with crypto. Most taxation policies demand a $200 exclusion amount per transaction when using foreign currency.

AVOID SCAMS

The prevalence of opportunistic con artists has been on the rise following the exponential growth of cryptocurrencies. Uncertainties around the regulation of cryptocurrencies coupled with their privacy have made the technology a breeding ground for fraudsters. Investors and traders are always urged to remain keen and vigilant while investing in any virtual currency scheme. First of all, they should evaluate the team behind a project, study the company and the utility of a given product. Also, you need to learn about historical scams and how history would repeat itself. Acquainting yourself with information about past scammers will help you identify potential frauds.

1. **Fake exchanges** - Following the 2017 bitcoin boom, most people were blinded by the promise of lucrative returns. Which made them less cautious of scams. A Korean fake exchange identifying itself as BitKRX positioned itself as the leading trading exchange in South Korea and ended up disappearing with funds.

2. **Bitcoin-based Ponzi schemes** - Back in 2019, a trio was charged in a fraud scheme worth $722 million after they solicited money from people with promises of shares on crypto mining pools. The scheme would also reward investors for recruiting new investors.

3. **Fake coins** - Fake ICOs and fake altcoins had become a norm between 2017 and 2018. One good example is Big Coin which allegedly ripped off customers $6 million worth of investment.

4. **Social engineering** - Someone could either email you or give you a call and position themselves as officers from the Internal Revenues Service.

They then demand that you should pay taxes immediately or send them money to prevent huge bans. These artists go a step further to demand payment in bitcoin or crypto to avoid being traced back.

5. **Malware** - Cybercriminals are penetrating through user accounts and crypto storage wallets by stealing login information through malware. Most victims download malware into their devices without knowing by innocently clicking a link or opening an email.

6. **Pump and Dump** - This has been a common phenomenon in the stock market since time immemorial. A group of con artists come together, invest large amounts of funds on a stock and in large numbers. Which drives the price of an asset high. Once the price rises and outsiders invest in the instrument, the perpetrators disappear with the money.

5

TRADING PSYCHOLOGY

E motional intelligence is what draws the line between the good trader and the great trader. You want to be a great trader. Because good could sometimes backslide to average and then to bad. But the great trader remains great.

Fundamental and technical analysis skills might be the prerequisite skills for all traders but emotional intelligence is the most important skill set. Trading psychology takes into account the discipline, risk management, and sober decision-making attributes associated with the success of a trader. The key definition of trading psychology according to Investopedia, describes the mental state at which a trader is able to draw concrete trading strategies and which determines whether a stock trader succeeds or fails.

As you read on, you will notice a couple of emotions that stand out when talking about trading psychology. Such emotions will include fear, hope, greed, and regret. You are also going to find out that in your everyday trading activities, a good mental balance is crucial. Trading securities requires one to make many complicated and swift decisions daily. These decisions should never be informed by greed, fear, hope, or regret. All traders set out in this venture with a solid trading strategy. This strategy should always be followed to the letter mainly because it's the lifeblood of your business, capital, and income. Trading around the aforementioned emotions forces one to deviate from their trading strategy. For example, greed could force one to change their pre-customized stop losses and targets. Thereby messing up their risk management plans, which could end up causing more losses and an inherent inability to take care of the emotions.

For instance, greed-driven trades could be characterized by high-risk trading, the buying of securities from an un-researched, untested venture. You might have observed that the securities of company X are growing rapidly in price and end up investing without undertaking a keen study on such companies. Some traders end up staying within a profitable trading position longer than they should mainly as a result of greed. This is because they are trying to squeeze out that extra coin or profit. Traders have squashed their investments as a result of greed more particularly and common during the final stage of bull markets. At this point, market speculation is at its highest and individuals forget their plans and dive into an investment without careful thinking.

Greed also compels the start of other unfavorable emotions such as impatience, regret, need for revenge, anger among others. All of which is bad for trading.

Regret gets in the way of trading when a trader misses out on a price surge and tends to move fast into a position. They do this while trying to consolidate their mishap and more than often, they will incur losses because prices tend to drop sharply after peaking high. Regret causes the fear of missing out or (FOMO), a very common name in the stock market.

And then there is fear. Fear occurs when the cryptocurrency market crashes and a trader attempts to jump in and save their funds from liquidation. This results in traders closing their positions without sticking to the plan. It is not advisable to close a trading position when concerned about a huge loss. Fear catalyzes panic selling and it's a dangerous emotion to have if you are embarking on being a great trader. In most cases, a trader in fear will cut winning positions scared of losing profits back, hold on to losing positions afraid of bearing the losses or hesitate to execute a trade because of an imminent loss.

The difference between trading and gambling is the hope for returns. Hope prevents traders from cutting their losses as they keep holding on to a position that could cause them heavy losses. Identify all hope factors that are getting in the way of your trading and eliminate them; before you end up destroying your capital funds.

GREAT TRADERS HAVE THESE PSYCHOLOGICAL ATTRIBUTES:

- They understand limits and avoid overtrading
- They always maintain a solid trading discipline
- They have in place a strategic risk management plan
- They always follow their plan.

Remember that a good mental state is important to undertake sober technical analysis. The majority of great traders rely on interpreting charts to make their decisions. Charts are a good way to study market patterns and forecast the future movement of a digital asset. These charts help you identify trends and spot buying/selling opportunities. Meanwhile, a firm grasp of market fundamentals, intuition, and understanding are crucial; and all come from the wellness of trading psychology.

Below are tips on how to strengthen your trading psychology and grow your profits:

1. **Understand your personality** - Are you that guy who's always impulsive, or the stoic one who doesn't fall for emotions? Knowing your personality will help you control your emotions beforehand. For example, an impulsive person knows they can be overcome by greed/fear. Hence they will be in a better position to hold back when such emotions arise.

2. **Create a solid trading plan** - Customize a trading plan and stick to it. Know beforehand the amount of time you are putting in, the capital you will bring in, and what technical indicators you will rely on. And don't let emotions get in the way of your trading strategy. Follow it to the book.

3. **Be patient** - Do not expect profits right from the start. Appreciate small payouts while starting and don't get upset when you make a loss. Open positions one step at a time, be patient, be persistent.

4. **Avoid greed** - Read, read, and read. Acquire extensive knowledge of market patterns and always know the market might sometimes be out of your

favor. Adapt new trading strategies, avoid greed, and be prepared for losses.

WHAT DOES IT HAVE TO DO WITH TRADING?

Trading psychology gives you the right mindset to conduct sober trading activities. This helps you lessen the implications of market biases and emotions. Therefore, giving you the advantage to beat the market and make a profit.

What are the Benefits of Psychological Trading?

Let's take a look at why psychological trading is important and why you should always have a sober mental state while conducting crypto trading activities.

1. Psychological Trading Helps You Set Rules

All business ventures require sound rules and regulations. Treat your trading activities as a business. Have careful plans, stick to these plans, and have in place rules. Embark on following these rules to the letter. A good approach to customizing your own rules is first understanding your risk-reward tolerance. Understand when you need to open a trade and when you should close the trade. Customize stop losses and profit targets. Stick to this and prevent emotions from getting in the way of your strategy. Plan out what events you are going to look at that could influence your trading decisions either directly or indirectly.

2. Remaining Flexible

Having a sober mental state will help you remain flexible and open to new ideas. You will research, understand market patterns, and experiment with techniques. In the long run, you will have widened your perspective, understanding, and knowledge of the market. You will have better options for risk management and mitigating loss. As a matter of fact, you will be able to avoid emotional biases while making trading decisions.

3. Psychological Trading will Help you Conduct Research

A good mental balance will put you in good shape to study patterns. You will devote as much time to strategizing that will help make informed decisions. You will further your understanding of macroeconomics and get to understand technical analysis. In fact, you are going to attend seminars, watch webinars, and enroll in groups that help you learn. Your passion for the art of trading will grow day by day, and you are going to be a successful trader. Sound knowledge is crucial in helping you avoid emotions such as fear and regret.

4. Psychological Trading will Help you Overcome Greed

A famous Wall Street quote warns investors against greed. The saying goes something like, "Bulls make money, bears make money but pigs get slaughtered". Traders should never get into the habit of opening trading positions inspired by greed. A trend reversal could cut your profits down when you hold on to a gain position for too long. Your trading plan should always be based on the foundations of rational thinking and informed thinking. Identify instincts of greed and eliminate them. Develop your strategies by sticking to knowledge, market patterns, and fundamental analysis.

TRADING ISSUES THAT DEAL WITH THE PSYCHE

Learning and understanding psychological trading will prevent you from acting within the boundaries of any of the following biases:

1. **Negative bias** - This bias is based on an emotional response that makes you always focus on the negative aspects of a trade. It makes you hardly focus on what could work out, or what aspects of a strategy could go right. Therefore, forcing most traders to abandon a complete trading strategy

without experimenting with it. Without a negative bias, one would have tweaked the strategy slightly instead of completely scrapping it off.

2. **Representative bias** - The representative bias forces traders to replicate trading strategies that worked out in the past. This results in opening positions without conducting prior analysis, research, and carefully thinking about the trades. Since you are inclined that the technique will work out as it did in the past. Remember the dynamics of crypto markets (and even the stock market) are ever-changing. Each market instance demands its approach and careful planning.

3. **Status quo** - Trading, especially cryptocurrency trading is a nascent, exponentially growing industry. As the great trader you are, ensure you learn and explore new ways of trading. Identify and practice new and viable trading strategies. Embrace technologies and stop hanging on to old trading techniques.

4. **Confirmation bias** - Some traders will go out looking for information, analysis, and predictions that confirm their pre-drafted strategies and ideas. Usually, the confirmation bias makes them ignore or disregard information and predictions that don't support their ideas.

5. **Gambler's fallacy** - Do not dare to assume that an asset will continue with an uptrend just because it's increasing. Security markets are not that predictable. They require careful planning. Stick to your targets and stop losses. And don't be greedy.

Also, check out the bullet list below to identify some of the compulsions that biased trading will cause:

- Fear of taking losses/being stopped
- Closing trades too early
- Averaging down or continuing a losing position
- Hoping and wishful thinking
- Compulsive trading inspired by market excitement or addiction
- Excessive joy after winning a position
- Limiting profits
- Failure to follow your trading strategy
- Second-guessing and overthinking
- Failure to trade the right position size
- You will trade in excess
- Scared of trading
- Irritable and regretful, you will even want to revenge losses like gamblers
- You might end up trading with borrowed money, loans, or money you can't afford to lose.

Once you fully understand the importance of mental wellbeing to trading, you will become aware of how it could influence your trading success. Awareness alone is crucial when improving an activity, or how you conduct business. Technical analysis will never cheat you into opening a position. What is often wrong is how you approach technical analysis, your perception, and the decision that perception will inspire. If it will inspire a biased decision, then you are fated to fail. Chances are more and more losses will kill your trading passion, you will become a bad trader and you will end up closing business. You won't even try another day because your decision to trade is now suffering from the roadblocks of fear, impatience, and regret. You won't even get the chance to become a good trader. Yet all I wish for you is to become the greatest trader there could ever be.

AVOID EMOTIONAL TRADING

This chapter aims to help you break the patterns of emotional trading and embrace critical thinking and careful analysis when you set out to trade. The trading world is full of advice, guidance, and motivation from trading coaches. While I am not insinuating that most of this advice is wrong, sometimes you might find it hard to adapt to some of their taught styles. Have an open mind but remain aware that some of the strategies offered by professional traders are highly personalized to suit their needs, preferences, and style. And mostly might not work out for you. Nonetheless, a good way to set out in the trading world is by employing universally accepted techniques. Such techniques include:

- Keeping off demo trading
- Employing stop-loss orders
- Setting goals and pre-trading rules

But why should one avoid demo trading? Especially given the feature was created for people to learn how to trade and practice in a virtual environment. Well, demo trading is by design meant to help a beginner learn how to trade, curb emotions, and understand the interface of a trading environment. However, a demo account is only applicable where a beginning trader lacks the overall experience to trade and doesn't have much capital to spend on learning. The problem with a demo account is it will never teach you how to properly manage your risks. By virtual, losing and winning virtual funds isn't similar to losing or winning real cash. Real cash makes you think, carefully plan out your strategy, and finally get to analyze the markets in the right way.

Stop orders on the other hand come in handy to the busy and emotionally impulsive trader. This feature ensures one can curb their greed, gain control over their trades and follow up with a strategy. The trade closes when the profits hit a certain target or when losses hit a certain point. Stop orders are beneficial if you are aspiring to avoid emotional trading, on your way to become a great trader.

The next important thing is setting your goals. Create a definite trading plan alongside the goals you wish to achieve. A good way to calculate and pre-determine your goal is to express your values as percentages. The goal should extend between 6 - 12 months. If something happens out of the blue, you will always have a backup plan depending on your goals.

A great trader will always stand out. Among the key things determining their ability to outshine the market is their routine. A pre-trading ritual is usually the thing a trader does before starting their trades. Perhaps it could be kicking off the day with a mug of coffee, reading the newspaper, studying analysis articles on financial blogs, or jogging. All these things enable one to start their trading activities with a positive mindset. Such a mindset is crucial to establish a confident strategy and help keep your emotions under control. Again, avoid having too much confidence that will end up graduating into greed.

FIVE WAYS TO IMPROVE YOUR MINDSET

Like a soldier always sharpens his sword for a battle, always sharpens your mind for a trading session. This will improve your mindset and put you in good shape to grow as a trader. So how do you improve your mindset?

Here are five tips to follow.

1. **Learn and Keep Learning** - The only way to create a solid positive mindset is to learn and understand cryptocurrency markets. Take your time to grasp the fundamentals of the market, study charts, understand price movements, reversals, and market reactions to certain socio-political and economic events. Embrace new technology, adopt tools to boost your productivity, and never stop believing in the value of education in making informed trading decisions. Valuable market information will help create insight-driven and actionable trading strategies.

2. **Put losses in Control** - Have a way to manage your losses. Don't let the losses cross the lines and eat up your capital. This is a big problem for newbie traders who wait for a loss to graduate into profitable gains. Hence they fail to close the trade when it amasses huge amounts of loss, mainly

because they fail to admit their trading strategy might have problems.

3. **Remain sober, remain present** - have your full attention to the activity at hand. Don't wander elsewhere while conducting your trades. Let's face it, you might be overloaded with news, insights, data, and advice. All these might pose problems as you attempt to filter out between what's right and what's wrong. It's also important to focus on the trades. Don't rely on past trades and even if you do so, review those past trades systematically and methodologically. Relate the events and fundamentals of the past trades with current events.

4. **Understand your Limits** - Avoid overtrading. Don't overstay when other traders have long closed their sessions. There is a line between working hard and overworking. Overworking will rip you off the mental well-being to take on the next trading session. Earlier we mentioned the need to learn about your personality. Have your weaknesses and strengths at your fingertips. Know under which conditions or environment you are certainly going to perform maximally and what inhibits your decision-making process. Avoid impulsion. Stay cool and don't trade beyond what you can afford.

Avoid trading with borrowed money as much as you can and keep risks at bay through a solid risk management plan.

5. **Maintain a Trading Journal** - cover all aspects of your trading activities on a daily basis by writing them in a diary. Include the details that matter. What inspired that profit on Monday, what led to the loss you incurred on Tuesday, and so on. Always update the entries in your journal and make notes of market analysis. Write down the profits or losses of every trading session, include comments and insights into what led to certain positions.

The art of psychological trading is crucial in the cryptocurrency market. Particularly given the excitement that's currently characterizing digital assets. The industry has made some overnight billionaires but it doesn't mean this could be the same for you. Avoid the fear of missing out and take the time to understand the basic market fundamentals that are relevant to your area of trade.

III

LEARNING TO TRADE

6

THE FIRST STEP

THE FIRST STEP

Any kind of trader must first choose a reputable company that offers exchange services and a wallet. From this point, what follows is as simple as getting every document right and being verified. Different websites have in place varying mechanisms for verifying users. For some companies, it's as easy as an email confirmation. Others you will need to provide 2-factor authentication using your mobile phone and email. And then there are those exchanges that push its verification process a notch higher by adhering to Know your customer (KYC) policies. Such an exchange will verify your identity by asking for an Identification Card, driver's license, or passport.

It's important to have a good secure wallet. Not all exchanges provide a cold storage wallet. Therefore, consider other options. Good examples of quality wallets include Atomic, Trezor, and Metamask. But you will also find that most cryptocurrencies in the market provide their own official wallets. Ethereum has MyEtherWallet, Bitcoin has Bitcoin Core Wallet, there is Dash Core and Litecoin-QT.

In Summary, a cryptocurrency trader must have all the following in place:

- Personal Identification documents
- Secure internet connection
- Payment method
- Profile on a cryptocurrency exchange
- Personal wallet, cold storage is advisable.

Valid payment methods for a crypto trader include debit/credit cards, bank accounts, wire transfers, and payment applications such as PayPal and Payoneer. Also remember to take note of your withdrawal method, after getting the coins. It turns out the means of withdrawing funds from some exchanges is a problem and you need to figure this out early in the process. Some other withdrawal methods include specialized Bitcoin and Bitcoin Cash ATMs, as well as specialized local Peer-to-Peer exchanges.

Take note that cryptocurrency ATMs require you to submit government-issued IDs and become verified.

Credit/debit cards supporting 3D secure are the only ones that can buy crypto. Keep this in mind and the process of pre-funding your account will be flawless. Contact the issuing institution and establish whether your card supports 3D Secure. Besides, you could also add it to your exchange account and see whether it works. In case of error messages, the card does not support 3D secure.

Know your Customer Exchange Policies

Know your customer regulations require a broker/platform to know and keep record of essential information about each customer. This policy aims at protecting both a broker and a customer. It's an ethical requirement in the securities industry and is being implemented across cryptocurrency platforms. There are three basic components of the KYC rule:

1. CIP or Customer Identification Program
2. Customer Due Diligence
3. Ongoing Monitoring

Customer Identification Program

Is your client who they say they are? The world prevalence rate for identity theft is high and has affected over 16.7 million citizens in the United States. According to Trulio.com, the US lost over $16.8 billion through identity theft and impersonification in 2017. The role of the Customer Identification Program is to ensure an individual conducting a financial transaction has their identity validated. This helps in curbing terrorism funding, money laundering, illicit activities, and corruption.

Customer Due Diligence

The next KYC procedure is ensuring your client is trustworthy and cannot engage in illegal activities. This step also ensures a platform is effectively managing its risks and keeping off potential threats, Politically Exposed Persons (or PEPs), terrorists, and criminals. All of which is a threat to funds and customer data. There are three levels of customer due diligence, these are; Simplified Due Diligence, Enhanced Due Diligence, and Basic Due Diligence.

Ongoing Monitoring

Platforms have in place oversight features for monitoring the activities of a customer. This could be on an ongoing basis and is developed on the basis of a given customer's risk profile. Factors that are usually taken into consideration while evaluating risk profile include:

- Activity spikes
- Unusual cross-border transactions
- Transacting with people on sanction lists
- Mentions in Adverse media

All blockchain transactions are publicly recorded. This means anyone on the blockchain can see which public addresses have large amounts of funds. The only advantage is they cannot put names and faces behind the public addresses. This makes transactions completely confidential and private; however, these transactions are not anonymous. Because they are linked to your identifying public address. Intelligence can easily trace them back to you. Crypto holders are usually advised to never reveal their private addresses. But it's also important to never reveal their public addresses. Because this would make them potential baits, especially if they hold huge amounts of cryptocurrencies.

Also, when creating exchange accounts and wallets, use secure internet practices. These include 2-factor authentication, unique and long alphanumeric passwords with special characters, and mixed capitalization.

CRYPTOCURRENCY EXCHANGE

A cryptocurrency exchange service will allow you to trade digital currencies and digital assets. You can hold, buy, or sell crypto through these exchanges. There are so many exchanges out there and landing on the right one can be hectic. There are three types of exchanges, centralized exchanges, decentralized exchanges, and peer-to-peer exchanges. All these exchanges provide users with the ability to trade digital currencies. There are several factors one should keep in mind when choosing an exchange platform. These factors are crucial for making informed choices. Let's have a look at each one of them.

1. **Geo-restrictions** - Most crypto exchange platforms have geographical restrictions and trading on them is illegal. Therefore, always make sure an exchange platform is legal in your country. Sometimes governments can crack your IP's ability to access and utilize a particular cryptocurrency exchange. When considering this fact, think about proper licensing and certification. What are the laws and regulations guiding practices in blockchain and crypto?

2. **Trade volumes and Liquidity** - Large trade volumes are the only indicator of liquidity.

Liquidity is usually an important factor for traders because, at the end of the day, they will need to change from fiat to crypto, vice versa. Leading centralized exchanges have an advantage because they command large amounts of users, and the liquidity is extremely unparalleled. At times you are not going to find all the coins you need on a given exchange. For example, some coins are too small for listing, others cannot afford the high listing fees of major exchanges. Therefore, you will need to join a decentralized exchange or smaller exchange to find them.

3. **Support Team** - All financial services require a good support team that promptly responds to queries on a 24/7 basis. If you come across a problem, the support should answer your inquiry as fast as possible.

4. **Security and Anonymity** - A good exchange should have strong security practices. The major exchanges command huge amounts of money, within the billions of dollars brackets. Therefore, security should be a priority for all of these exchanges.

5. **Google authentication or 2-Factor authentication** - These authentication methods prevent unauthorized persons from accessing your

account. By combining both of them, your account becomes fully secured and protected from potential criminals.

The Role of a Cryptocurrency Exchange

Exchanges facilitate the trading of cryptocurrencies. They provide liquidity to the industry by giving holders a platform to sell or buy digital currencies. Quality exchanges are usually user-friendly and have a well-designed user interface. Some centralized exchanges go a step further in helping their customers understand the ins and outs of trading. Majority of which will have a detailed blog page with an informative Frequently Asked Questions (FAQ) section. Exchanges also come in handy when providing a safe platform for one to transfer value through cryptocurrencies. They facilitate such transactions by also adding extra layers of reliability, security, speed, and convenience. Some such as Binance have numerous discounts which they send to their users through periodical newsletters.

Examples of Quality Exchanges

We have mentioned what factors make a good exchange. Putting those factors into consideration, we came up with the following list of exchanges.

1. Binance

2. Coinbase
3. Gemini
4. Kraken
5. Huobi

Alternatively, when buying cryptocurrencies, you could also use a cryptocurrency ATM. Which also acts as an in-person digital currency exchange. The ATMs allow you to insert cash into their system and use it to buy digital assets. And then the amount is transferred to a secure crypto wallet. Recently, the prevalence of Bitcoin ATMs is growing at a high rate. Finally, you can connect your local payment method with a Peer-to-Peer (P2P) exchange such as Localcrypto and LocalBitcoins to purchase or sell cryptocurrencies. LocalCryptos supports Litecoin, Ethereum, Dash, and Bitcoin. It includes a listing of buyers and sellers to choose from. And you can choose from whoever trading partner you want.

CONNECTING YOUR EXCHANGE

Below we are going to cover the various payment options you can link to cryptocurrency exchanges. These payment options facilitate the funding of your account with fiat and as a withdrawal medium for cashing out.

1. **PayPal** - PayPal allows clients to link their PayPal account with a cryptocurrency hub. While connecting both services, one has to provide the following details about themselves: physical address, taxpayer identification number, and date of birth. Somewhere during the process, you will have to verify your identity by submitting a copy of your government-issued Identification Card or any evidence of your place of residence, such as utility bills.

2. **Banks** - You can utilize a bank transfer to facilitate the purchase of cryptocurrencies from an exchange. Banks are popular for processing payments instantly.

3. **Credit/debit cards** - You could also use a debit/credit card to instantly recharge your exchange account directly from your bank account.

In case you are planning to engage in huge transactions, exchanges are going to ask for more identification information. This additional layer of verification serves to protect you, your funds, and your future relationship with the platform.

DETERMINING THE PRICES AND HOW TO PURCHASE

Trading in cryptocurrencies is different from trading in traditional currencies. Note that cryptocurrencies are not issued by central banks, they have no backing from the government and are typically not influenced by monetary policies, inflation rates, and economic growth indicators. Ideally what influences the value and price of cryptocurrencies are the following factors:

1. Forces of supply and demand of a particular digital currency
2. The cost associated with the creation of a digital currency, e.g. mining costs
3. Amount of reward awarded to a cryptocurrency miner after validating blockchain transactions
4. How many cryptocurrencies is a coin competing against?
5. The exchange you are conducting your trade on
6. Government regulations around the trading of a particular cryptocurrency
7. Internal governance.

Investing in a digital currency demands one to have the ability to make comparisons between a coin's current trading value and its intrinsic value. This helps an investor to understand when a given currency is overvalued or undervalued.

Intrinsic value is the value of a digital currency that's been determined through fundamental analysis and without having to refer back to its market value.

- Market value is the price at which a digital asset is currently being sold or bought in the actual market. The following are factors used to establish the intrinsic value of a cryptocurrency:
- Market/Use Case - what value do a given digital currency and its blockchain bring? What problems are they solving? How big is the problem and what is their revenue model?
- Community of Users - Does a digital currency command a large, supportive, and active community? What is the rate of growth of the community?
- The team behind a cryptocurrency project - Are the developers experienced? What's their background and how knowledgeable are they? Do they have the ability to lead a successful project?
- Funding - How a project is funded goes a long way in influencing the direction of a digital currency.

So, while establishing the intrinsic value of a given cryptocurrency, consider asking yourself the above questions. And once you have this, visit charting websites such as Yahoo Finance and Tradeview to conduct both technical and fundamental analysis. This will help you establish the market value of a digital currency and help you determine its future direction.

GOT YOUR WALLET

Once you have your preferred cryptocurrency exchange in place, you need somewhere to store your funds. Exchanges are not the safest places for storing your funds. There exist so many services offering wallet services; what you need is a reputable service with robust security features and a dedicated support team. Let's have a look at what to keep into consideration when choosing a cryptocurrency wallet.

1. **Cross compatibility** - A good wallet should support different devices from Android, IOS, Windows, and macOS. A cross-compatible wallet ensures flexibility and mobility of the application as you change from one device to another.

2. **Strong security features** - Consider a wallet with good security features such as 2-factor

authentication, multi-signature logins, passphrases, fingerprint features, or Pin Codes.

3. **Complete control of your private key** - Choose a wallet that gives you full control and access to your private key. Protect this private key with all your life.

Digital currency wallets are classified into two primary groups: Hot and Cold Storage Wallets.

Hot Wallets

Hot wallets require an internet connection. They are considered secure due to the online mechanisms and therefore vulnerable to cybercriminals. However, they are more accessible, portable, and user-friendly.

Cold Wallets

Cold wallets are offline and do not require an internet connection. They are highly secure and an extremely safe means of storing your funds. These wallets are ideal for investors holding large amounts of cryptocurrencies.

These wallets are further divided into the following five categories:

1. **Full Node Wallet** - These wallets host a

complete copy of the blockchain and give you control over your private key.

2. **Desktop wallet** - This wallet has a direct link between the cryptocurrency and the client.

3. **Custodial wallet** - These wallets are usually hosted on exchange platforms and do not give you control over your private keys.

4. **Mobile wallet** - These are wallets that are designed as mobile applications and are run through smartphones.

5. **Software wallet**

6. **Online Wallet** - A wallet whose data is held within a virtual/real server. Encryption of data is entrusted to the server.

7. **Paper wallet** - These are wallets that allow you to print the Quick response (QR) code of your associated public and private keys. Then you can digitally transact cryptocurrencies using a printed paper wallet.

8. **Hardware Wallet** - These are hardware devices designed to hold and secure cryptocurrencies. They could be memory cards or USB devices.

7

DAY TRADING 101

UNDERSTANDING DAY TRADING

An investor buys an asset in the early morning hours and sells it by the close of the day. You are a day trader if this is how you do it. For example, Ben wakes up in the morning and opens a trading position at 9:00 AM and closes this position by 6 PM on that very day. We can say Ben has executed a day trade. If Ben chose to close this position on the next day, this is no longer referred to as a Day Trade. Therefore, a position must be opened and closed within one day.

On a usual day, Ben capitalizes on short-term price movements on the cryptocurrency market by actively trading digital currencies. These price movements are catalyzed by market volatility. And the price of a digital currency must undergo short-term price movements at all times, for day trading to turn out successful. The length of these price movements determines how much profit or loss a trader is going to make.

Apart from cryptocurrencies, day trading takes place in other marketplaces. You can open a position on the stock market, close that position by the end of the day and cash out your profits. In fact, this method of trading is more common across stock markets and foreign exchange (forex).

The primary indicators that most day traders are sensitive about when making fast short-term trading decisions include announcements on interest rates, economic statistics, and corporate earnings. Market movements could sometimes be the result of the overall market psychology and the expectations of market participants. If those expectations are either exceeded or not met, the market's reaction is sudden and undergoes a significant price movement. A situation that poses a very good advantage for Day Traders.

What keeps a day trader going is their ability to exercise good risk management. This helps them maintain their losses within a small margin and their profits over a wider margin. Think of it as risk management. Placing capital at short-term risk with the aim of generating more money. And in case of slight mismanagement and eros in trading strategies, the system loses part of the capital and the trades become difficult to create a consistent source of income. The great day trader might sometimes have a predetermined entry position and exit position before they even execute a trade. Predefining positions help prevent emotions from taking the better part of a trading session. Besides, a trader will not have to spend much time overmanaging their positions.

At all times, the day trader aims at having a deep understanding of the market and some experience. Their ideas originate from good market analysis. Technical analysis (TA) comes in handy when pondering these ideas and making trading decisions. See, the position a trader opens or closes depends on their ability to interpret trading volumes, chart patterns, price action, and technical indicators. The ability to navigate across these factors calls for a crucial understanding of the market and essentially, good risk management skills.

Also, note, day traders, are never concerned with how fundamental events are going to influence their trading positions. This is usually because some fundamental events might implicate the market in the long term and might not come in handy during short-term trading The most popular trading pair on the stock market is the EUR/USD. However, BTC/USDT, BTC/ETH, ETH/LTC are the most popular trading pairs on the cryptocurrency market. The majority of day traders only trade one pair, the BTC/USDT. Others will customize their watchlist depending on the technical or fundamental aspects of digital security and choose the most favorable one.

According to an article entitled " Day Trading: Smart or Stupid" written by former Forbes Contributor *Neale Godfrey,* Day trading is preserved only for the few professional traders willing to stake huge amounts of capital, and which they can afford to lose. While this seems odd, it means one needs to have huge amounts of money to effectively capitalize on meager short-term price movements. The advantage of risk capital is wholly rewarding in the short term because a great day trader will never gamble on one trade using all their funds.

Out there, the majority of day traders are professionals working for huge financial management firms. These firms are known to spend lots of resources on training their day trading workforce. And usually, this training is world-class and supervised by experienced professionals. There is also the possibility of receiving personal mentorship from a trading coach. Furthermore, you will find their investment in cutting-edge trading technology and actionable insight acquisition is top class. The professionals are paid a base salary and awarded bonus commissions depending on their track record as traders of the firm. For example, TradingSim awards its employees 10-30% of the revenue they generate and a base salary of $50,000 - $70,000.

Then we have the individual day traders. They are on a lonely path but have a healthy capital backup that shields them from short-term risks. Their biggest advantage is an ability to familiarize themselves with stocks and a good understanding of the market. The individual trader grasps technical analysis indicators and knows how to interpret them. This trader has the ability to also implement emerging technology to their advantage, which helps them to understand trading volume, chart patterns, and price volumes. If you are planning to go in as an individual day trader, we recommend that you invest sufficient money to earn high gains from relatively tiny price movements. You are going to operate on a loss, in case you dip your toes in with less money and end up getting meager profits; which in the long run cannot even pay for the broker's commission.

Statistics around day trading are however not in favor of newbie traders. According to the aforementioned article, only 1% of intraday traders make a profit. Another estimation by Cointelegraph's Scott Melker indicates 95% of day traders fail. And let's have a look at a few more estimations that will prepare you psychologically when going into the trade of day trading:

1. **80 percent** of intraday traders quit within 1 -2 years.

2. Approximately **40 percent** day trade for only a month and then quit

3. Approximately **13 percent** go on with their trading activities after 3 years. And only 7 **percent** make it above 5 years.

Considering the following sinister statistics, let's answer your biggest question.

SHOULD I START DAY TRADING?

Before talking about whether or not you should be a day trader. Let's have a look at what entails this trade. The factors that consistent day traders rely on to keep going and the various strategies they employ to achieve a high win rate.

Factors to Consider when Day Trading

1. Liquidity of an Asset

The asset one chooses during day trading should be one that can effortlessly be exchanged for another asset and vice-versa. Day traders are reliant on short-term price movements, and they need to effortlessly sell an asset once it hits their target. Cryptocurrency markets have so many low liquidity assets and you need to avoid such trading pairs at all costs. Go for a crypto trading pair that has high liquidity, it will be easy to change hands and you will cash out gains made over small amounts of time.

2. Market Volatility

Market volatility is how fast or slow a currency is able to change in price. A highly volatile asset changes in price very frequently. A nonvolatile currency retains its price for an extended duration of time. Day traders take advantage of short-term but high price movements to make profits. The day traders use technical analysis to forecast the direction of a digital currency during an intraday session.

Successful day traders use the following factors to determine what assets to trade in and what positions to open or close. Below are the most popular strategies employed by these traders:

1. **Scalping** - Day traders believe that quick small profits can add up in the bulk of one's daily profits. The trader takes advantage of tiny price movements, makes tiny amounts of profits, and sells off faster. The day traders who use this method always have in place a committed and strict exit strategy. Mainly because a single big loss is likely to

reverse the impact of the small gains. Prerequisites to use scalping in your intraday trading are direct-access brokers, a live feed, and the mental ability to place and withstand small trades. Without adequate access to the right information, one will have a hard time making any considerable gains using scalping.

2. **Range Trading** - Trading range takes place when a digital currency trades consistently between a particular high and low for a duration of time. This enables a trader to define a range position within the prevailing structure. The trading position they open will initiate itself within the defined range, and the day trader only has to run the process until the asset moves out of the range. A prerequisite for range trading is being able to effortlessly interpret candlestick charts and momentum indicators. A good understanding of momentum indicators will deliver optimum results. Ideally, the top range in the trading range is considered the resistance, while the low range is essentially the support price.

3. **High-Frequency Trading (HFT)** - This trading method utilizes highly sophisticated automated trading algorithms to watch the asset markets and execute large buy/sell orders on behalf of the trader. The algorithms are popular for

analyzing multiple markets using preset conditions and executing high-speed trading positions. A prerequisite to using HFT in your day trading is to have large amounts of funds to support many small market positions.

Well, with that:

It turns out you can see how you can penetrate the art of day trading. So, let's look at the advantages of becoming an intraday trader.

Advantages of Day Trading

1. **Big quick money** - Day trading can help you generate lots of money within a small amount of time. But you shouldn't expect this to be quick. Take time, experiment, practice, and be consistent. Be patient and persistent until your trading strategy grows profit. Besides, a day trader has access to leverage. If you haven't heard about leverage, it's the ability to borrow money from a broker/ brokerage platform so that you can acquire additional digital assets or stocks.

2. **There are no fortnight risks** - Day trading ensures you do not postpone a trading session to the next day. Tuesday's risks are Tuesday's and

Monday's risks are Monday's. Many things could happen during a fortnight that could end up hurting your trading position. Any price drop in day trading is dangerous for day traders because this is likely to overturn the small profits.

3. **Day trading is simple** - You can start day trading with a small amount of money and be a better judge of the venture within a small amount of time. However, you need a good grasp of market knowledge and fundamentals. Understand these market factors, create a trading strategy, and remain consistent. You can start with little capital and capitalize on counting your profits over some time. Small capital will minimize associated risks and losses. But this is not saying you won't make losses.

4. **You can trade remotely** - Trading offers the optimum freelance lifestyle of being able to work from anywhere in the world. You can trade during your vacation remotely, in your bedroom, at home, or even in your office cubicle. If you love this lifestyle, consider becoming a day trader.

Disadvantages of Day Trading

1. **Stressful and frustrating** - The learning curve

for day traders is steep. As you learn, you are going to encounter losses. And these demands some level of persistence on your part to remain afloat. Manage your emotions, and don't let small losses get in the way of becoming a highly successful trader.

2. **Demands discipline** - You need to become more disciplined and focused. Set rules and let your trading goals align with these rules. Guard these rules with your life and always stick to the book. Do not place a trade out of greed and end up abandoning your outlined strategy. The average day trader opens lots of positions compared to the average securities investor. Therefore, you need a definite plan, and the discipline to stick to the plan.

3. **The mercy of High-Frequency Traders** - They say that any profit made by a trader is a subsequent loss by another trader within the market structure. Individual day traders might have to compete against losing to lucrative HFT traders who use sophisticated systems to place high-frequency positions.

4. **You can lose money quickly** - you are going to lose money and you are going to lose it within a very short amount of time. What you need to avoid is trading away your entire capital on one trade.

Allocate small lot sizes from your entire risk capital, diversify your trading pairs, and avoid overtrading. This way you are going to be bulletproof when it comes to loss and at the end of the day, you will be consistent, persistent, and among the 1% of day traders who make a profit.

QUALITIES OF A DAY TRADER

1. **Good day traders have mental toughness** - They are not scared and they don't feel demotivated when a trade loses. A good trader needs to bounce back in the event of loss and they shouldn't be frustrated when they fail. They expect much but frustration is never their potion.

2. **Good traders are adaptable** - Good traders can adapt to any market conditions. None of their trades will look similar and they will deal with multiple currency pairs and still remain successful. Quick price movements which are characteristic of day trading markets require a sharp flexible mind. Adaptability comes in handy when making quick decisions when a market changes.

3. **Good traders are independent** - The most profitable trades are made by traders who are independent thinkers. They learn and use the

insight to become creative and insightful. Being independent doesn't translate to doing everything on your own. There are times you will need help from professional mentors. In these circumstances, ask the right questions like how they come up with their strategies, the books they read, and how to become adaptable in a highly dynamic market. Build your own personal toolbox for opinions, and as Steve Jobs said, be hungry, be foolish.

DAY TRADING TERMINOLOGIES

1. **Pattern Day Trader Rules** - This rule adjudicates that a day trader is one that can take above 3 trades within a period of 5 days. The rule goes on to state that a day trader must always maintain a balance of $25,000 (minimum) in their trading account

2. **Swing Trading** - These are trades held during fortnights for at least 1 night.

3. **Bullish** - A bullish market is one where the price action is moving upwards.

4. **Bearish** - A bearish market is one where the price action is moving downwards.

5. **Day Trade** - A day trade takes place when a

person opens a trading position and closes that position within the same day.

6. **Lagging Indicator** - These are technical economic factors that are commonly associated with trailing the price action of a digital currency.

7. **Leading Indicator** - These are actionable economic indicators that get ahead of the normal economic cycle before the market forms a definite pattern.

8. **Crossed market** - A market structure where the bid price of a cryptocurrency is higher than the asking price.

HOW TO TRADE BITCOIN

WHY BITCOIN?

Applauded by its enthusiasts as a market-disrupting technology, Bitcoin is the most widely recognized and traded cryptocurrency in the universe. The novel cryptocurrency, perhaps the most polarizing in the financial market, has reached breathtaking heights since Satoshi Nakamoto introduced it in 2009.

History

Bitcoin was created and applied by Satoshi Nakamoto, who combined several existing ideas from the cypherpunk public. Bitcoin has rapidly grown to be a recognizable coinage both online and offline. Several businesses started accepting Bitcoin in addition to customary coinages in the middle

2010s. Bitcoin was originally listed as a domain in August 2008. In October 2008, a link to a paper titled Bitcoin authored by Nakamoto was sent to a cryptography mailing list.

Bitcoin is the leading cryptocurrency in terms of acceptance, total market capitalization, and trading volume. Bitcoin is the basis on which additional cryptocurrencies are measured. The primary objective of Bitcoin was to serve as a digitally encrypted coinage that can be used to pay for goods and services.

Investing in Bitcoin is exactly what it sounds like - using fiat currencies such as dollars and pounds to buy Bitcoin. Besides, it might also mean taking your retirement proceeds and investing them in an eligible Bitcoin IRA. Over the last ten years, Bitcoin's remarkable rise has enticed a new breed of investors. However, crypto remains a burgeoning asset class, and many aspiring investors are confused about where to commence.

Bitcoin trading can be an effective method of earning from the crypto market. If you closely watch the financial instruments provided by compliant brokers, you will note that Bitcoin and other digital assets are included in their tradable assets listing. Because of the increasingly rampant adoption of Bitcoin and its massive volatility, it has grown into a popular trading instrument among traders. Several reasons are backing why you should consider trading Bitcoin. Let us discuss them below:

1. Inflation Proof

Notably, Satoshi embedded 21 million coins restriction cap on the original Bitcoin code. That means Bitcoins' supply is scarce, and only 21 million coins will ever exist. Currently, 89 percent (18,680,475 BTC) of the total Bitcoin supply is in circulation, and only a little over 10 percent are yet to be mined. At the time of writing, the market value of Bitcoin is $60,673.37, slightly below its all-time high of $61,683 set on March 13, 2021.

Yes, the key reason why you should choose to invest in Bitcoin is because of its scarcity. This means that Bitcoin is specifically immune to inflation, except before the last coin is mined. Once all the 21 million tokens have been distributed through mining, they will become deflationary since no other Bitcoin will ever be produced. As a rule of thumb, supply-induced scarcity will occur with Bitcoins falling out of circulation as private keys are lost.

2. High Volatility

Volatility can be described as the rate at which price fluctuates up and down. Variations in market demand and supply are the reason behind such fluctuations. For instance, if the market demand for Bitcoin eclipses the supply,

Bitcoin's valuation tends to appreciate. On the contrary, when supply eclipses demand, the market valuation drops.

Every time the subject on the viability of Bitcoin as a payment means, store of value, and a unit of accounting arises, naysayers emphasize that the novel cryptocurrency is too volatile to carry out those roles. While there is some truth to such sentiments, Bitcoin's massive volatility is a positive side. Volatility provides investors, especially day traders and scalpers, with the opportunity to amplify their portfolio value.

Most naïve dealers do not comprehend the significance of market impulsiveness. If an individual wants to make steady profits, they should learn how to find and take full advantage of volatility. It would be best for an individual to learn about technical and fundamental analysis before trading Bitcoin. The subject of fundamental and technical analysis will be covered later in the book.

3. High Liquidity

In a nutshell, liquidity can be described as just how easy it is to exchange an asset for fiat. As more traders frequently trade an asset regularly, it becomes more liquid. Bitcoin's development curve from its early days until today demonstrates this. It was a challenging task to find people to buy your cryptocurrency for whichever amount of money during its early days. Those days are gone, and today, many exchanges have various traders who are ready to purchase or sell Bitcoin at any given time. Bitcoin is lauded as the most liquid financial asset owing to the global establishment of cryptocurrency exchange platforms.

Bitcoin traders and investors can easily exchange Bitcoin for cash or any other financial asset in real-time. The high liquidity provides Bitcoin traders with a feasible ecosystem to work with, especially for scalpers and day traders.

4. Increased Institutional Demand

On April 14, 2021, Bitcoin price reached a new all-time high after hitting $64,863.10. However, it is not guaranteed to stay on this level forever since its price can drop towards $20,000 within days as fast as it can hit a new all-time high. Bitcoin's increased market price can be attributed to institutional investors beginning to invest in Bitcoin as a hedge against inflation.

Earlier this year, Tesla injected $1.5 billion worth of liquidity into Bitcoin. Investment companies that never used to discuss investing in Bitcoin with their clients have now begun doing so. Bitcoin's historical rally since late 2020 was partly driven by the entry of large institutional investors into the market. 2020 will always be remembered as the year Bitcoin drew the attention of mainstream institutional investors. With the ever-growing mainstream institutional adoption of Bitcoin, it is reason enough to believe in the flagship cryptocurrency.

PICKING YOUR PLATFORM

Bitcoin trading has become more mainstream over the years, and this has triggered the emergence of more and more trustworthy trading and exchange platforms. As such, anybody with a few dollars to invest and a burning desire to succeed can start trading Bitcoin or any other digital currency. Understanding how to purchase and sell Bitcoin is a critical step in joining the cryptocurrency market.

To trade Bitcoin, you need to join an exchange platform that supports Bitcoin trading. Selecting an exchange platform that favorably complements your Bitcoin trading needs is the most significant initial step.

What is an exchange?

An exchange platform is a digital marketplace that facilitates the buying and selling of cryptocurrencies such as Bitcoin using fiat currency or other altcoins. The primary function of a crypto exchange platform is to ensure transparent and organized trading. The other role is to efficiently disseminate price information for any crypto assets trading on that particular exchange.

Bitcoin exchanges tend to match buyers and sellers and generate their profit by charging trading commissions and transaction fees. Different crypto exchanges have different ways of depositing funds, such as credit/debit cards, bank transfers, mobile money transfers, gift cards, or even money orders. Traders can also access different withdrawal methods supported by the platforms such as PayPal, bank transfer, Skrill, cash delivery, or even check to mail.

There are several factors to consider before joining a cryptocurrency exchange platform. A trader's biggest concern is the security of their funds. Selecting the wrong exchange platform can lead down a path filled with wasted effort and funds. Before choosing an exchange, it would be best to conduct due diligence and thorough research. So, what are the factors or features you should look at before joining an exchange?

- **Security**: If you will be making large volume transactions, you want assurance that your assets will be safe. The first thing to look at before joining an exchange is the security features provided by the platform.
- **The number of supported assets**: There are more than 1,500 different cryptocurrency projects in existence. Apart from Bitcoin, you want to know the number of supported cryptos by a particular

exchange. Portfolio diversification is essential when investing in cryptocurrencies, and you don't want to put all your eggs in one basket.

- **Fees and commission**: The main reason for trading Bitcoin is to generate profit. The amount of commission charged per every trade will ultimately impact your profit margin or the extent of the loss. You should compare and contrast the commission charged by various crypto trading platforms before joining.

- **User experience:** Newbies in the cryptocurrency landscape need a platform that is easy to operate. Easy-to-use platforms with fantastic user experience draw in the most significant trading volumes.

After conducting your research and settling on one platform, you will be required to sign up with the exchange and undergo a whole range of verification processes to verify your identity. The verification process is commonly referred to as KYC (know your customer). After successful registration and verification, you can now deposit funds in your account and experience the world of cryptocurrency trading.

Exchange Platforms Suitable for Day Trading

The exchanges should offer three vital benefits; cold storage, robust safety with two-factor confirmation, and linked safe wallets. Day trading Bitcoin can be very lucrative due to the massive volatility. To successfully day trade Bitcoin, you need to join the most liquid crypto exchange platform that offers instant execution. Some of the best exchange platforms for day trading include:

Coinbase

Coinbase was established in 2012, precisely three years after the release of the Bitcoin code by Satoshi. The platform is the biggest in the United States, hosting over twenty million users. It is famous for its easily understandable cryptocurrency swapping platform, Coinbase Pro. Coinbase supports more than 25 distinct cryptocurrencies for swapping like Bitcoin, Ethereum, and Litecoin.

Pros

1. High liquidity
2. Wide variety of crypto options
3. Easy to use

Cons

1. User doesn't control private keys
2. High fees when not using Coinbase Pro version

eToro

Etoro is perfect for day trading because it provides zero-commission crypto, stock, and ETF trading and access to copy trading. The UK-based platform has over 15 million account holders from more than 100 different nations.

It does not offer the same range of investments as traditional brokers, has hidden fees, and education is sub-par. eToro crypto offers sixteen distinct coins.

Pros

1. Wide variety of altcoins
2. Social trading with a vast community of crypto traders
3. Easy to operate

Cons

1. Wide spreads
2. A minimum amount of $25 set to buy Bitcoin

Kraken

It was established in 2011. It provides support for 18 distinct cryptocurrencies apart from Bitcoin; Ripple, Monero, and Dash. Currently, Kraken provides a web platform but lacks a mobile app.

Pros

1. Very safe exchange with 2FA
2. Reasonable trading commission and withdrawal fees
3. Sleek user experience
4. Proof of reserves audit

Cons

1. Not beginner-friendly
2. Sophisticated charts and symbols
3. Only wire transfer withdrawals

Bittrex

It was established in 2014 in Washington and boasts more than $1 billion daily in trading volume. It provides over 100 tradable currencies; Bitcoin, Ethereum, and Litecoin. However, it lacks a mobile app or desktop.

Pros

1. Requires few verification details
2. Faster verification
3. Very secure

Cons

1. It doesn't support leveraged and margin trading
2. Sluggish client support
3. It does not support fiat currencies

Gemini

It was established by the Winklevoss twins in the year 2015. It is an authorized digital asset exchange and custodian suitable for both persons and organizations. It offers the Gemini Dollar and permits users to purchase, sell, and stock; Bitcoin, Litecoin, Ethereum ZCash, and Bitcoin Cash.

Pros

1. Fast verification
2. Very secure
3. Provides both IOS and Android platforms
4. Low fees

Cons

1. Transactions less than $200 attract high fees
2. Manual approval to join Gemini's ActiveTrader

Robinhood

Robinhood was established back in 2014 but recently added support for cryptocurrencies in 2018. It is suitable for individuals who trade a diverse set of assets. The Robinhood cryptocurrency platform permits traders to swap Ethereum, Bitcoin, Bitcoin SV, Litecoin, Dogecoin, and Ethereum Classic.

Pros

1. Easy to use and attractive user interface
2. Low fees
3. Altcoin variety

Cons

1. Lack of transparency about prices
2. Geographical restrictions

STEP-BY-STEP BITCOIN TRADING

The first step will be opening an account with a suitable Bitcoin exchange platform. Generally, most of these platforms, as discussed earlier, have an easy onboarding and verification process. After creating an account with a broker of your choice, you can follow the following steps to trade Bitcoin successfully:

Choose a trading strategy.

One should select a strategy depending on their availability, capital spent, experience level, and discipline. You can choose one of the following trading strategies:

- **Day trading**: In this strategy, you buy and sell Bitcoin within the same day taking advantage of price swings.
- **Swing trading**: Swingers use different techniques to speculate Bitcoin price movements ranging from a couple of days to several weeks.
- **Scalp trading**: Scalping is a short-term intraday Bitcoin trading strategy that takes advantage of small price swings.
- **Auto trading**: Automated Bitcoin trading involves automated trading robots that utilize advanced algorithms and technologies such as

machine learning and artificial intelligence to buy and sell Bitcoin profitably.

Developing the trading plan

After choosing a strategy, you can start expounding the Bitcoin trading layout. A trading layout helps individuals make trading decisions based on the information they have gathered before entering a trade. From this, a person can make knowledgeable decisions that enable them to avoid getting into or exiting a trade early or late. In this connection, follow the tips below when laying out your trading plan:

- Define your short-term and long-term goals.
- Propose several reasonable financial risks for every trade.
- Suggest a risk-reward ratio to validate the risk you are willing to take for each trade.
- Choose the types of Bitcoin markets you will enter, for instance, binary options.

Researching the Markets

The Bitcoin market is constantly changing and does not remain the same for long. As Bitcoin adoption expands, the cryptocurrency landscape is continuously evolving and developing. Owing to this, conducting sufficient research is vital before you begin trading.

You should read cryptocurrency news regularly to stay on top of every update. Learn the applications of Bitcoin, and track the daily highs and lows.

Trading and Monitoring

The next step is to place a Bitcoin trade. This procedure involves entering the amount of capital you are willing to stake on a trade and defining an exit plan.

You will need to apply position sizing and risk management alternatives such as "stop-loss" and "take-profit" orders. This gives you greater control of the trade.

RISKS AND HOW TO AVOID THEM

Threat of Crypto Cyber Crime

The potential of anonymously using Bitcoin to commit cybercrimes with more excellent protection has become a theme that traders have to deal with. Although the industry is becoming sophisticated day by day, crimes are still serious risks. Crypto-jacking, fake cryptocurrency token sales, and hacking are some of the most notorious cybercrimes.

The risk can be avoided using the security tools available to either mitigate or permanently eliminate them. The security tools include using cryptocurrency hardware wallets, updated security software, and proper storage of private keys by writing it down on a piece of paper or storing it in a hardware wallet.

Mishandling Private Keys

Storing your Bitcoin safely is essential. When you own Bitcoin, you own the private key to the Bitcoin network. Whoever has private keys can control the Bitcoins, and if your private keys fall into the wrong hands, your Bitcoin can be stolen.

Choosing an Insecure Trading Platform

All cryptocurrency exchange platforms, including the most renowned ones, face the risk of being hacked. For instance, the Binance $40 million hack back in 2019 surprised many people. If it happened to Binance, it could happen to anyone.

There is no guarantee that an exchange cannot be hacked. However, more time can be spent researching alternatives available, their security system, and their track records. Exchanges that provide solid security measures include Kraken's, PrimeXBT's, and Coinbase.

Trading on FOMO and FUD

Unscrupulous and ill-intentioned individuals have taken advantage of the tidal wave of beginners. When you open a trade based on emotions instead of analysis, there is a huge possibility you will lose capital.

A good trader should do sufficient research to gain a deeper understanding of market movements. You should develop a trading strategy with indicators and guidelines that you perceive. Follow the recent news in the crypto world, and avoid trading on rumors.

TOP FOUR MISTAKES YOU SHOULD AVOID

1. Using Wrong Tools

Some cryptocurrency tools were not designed with day trading in mind and can limit an individual's ability to swap efficiently. For instance, wallets like Trezor and Ledger have total security features but are not meant for regular trading. Signing and confirming transactions from such wallets take time, and this would cause an individual to be late for swaps they were waiting for.

Mitigation

An individual should store the cryptocurrency on the swapping platform they use for regular trading. The individual should look for safety tools available in standard trading platforms; whitelisting and U2F support.

2. Entering a Position, one can't Exit.

Sometimes an individual can get into a trade that is hard to exit. Some illiquid crypto exchange platforms may have low exchanging volumes if one is swapping on the weekend or during a holiday. The situation can make one lose the opportunity to take profits.

Mitigation

The individual should avoid trading in times of low liquidity in cryptocurrency. One may utilize the liquidity they have by swapping on exchanges that allow them to access multiple exchanges simultaneously.

3. Overemphasizing

This occurs when an individual ignores what is happening in the market and focuses on the technical indicators. For example, an individual can have a trading plan that utilizes differentials in correlated cryptocurrencies like BTC and ETH. In this scenario, the technical examination could be the downfall of the individual who recently purchased positions that are dropping.

Mitigation

An individual should keep on reading crypto broadcasts and analyzing prices. The news helps the individual to stay updated about the market conditions. An individual should also set "stop-loss orders" to mitigate losses in case of contagion.

4. Lack of Proper Hedging Strategies

Risk management is the most vital of regular trading. For example, an individual watching a Bitcoin chart can identify many Doji candlesticks and decide to purchase more Bitcoin. Unfortunately, Bitcoin's price swings in the opposite direction, and they lose money.

Mitigation

You can mitigate this by diversifying your trading portfolio. Apart from Bitcoin, there are other very profitable altcoins in the market. Investing in a variety of assets helps you maintain your capital.

9

TRADING IN YOUR ETHEREUM

ETHEREUM AS A WHOLE

Ethereum is a digital platform that enables developers to build a broad array of decentralized applications ranging from voting systems, security programs, to payment methods. In the same vein as Bitcoin, Ethereum functions outside the injunction of sovereigns such as governments and financial authorities.

The basic concept behind the creation of Ethereum was created by Russian-Canadian programmer Vitaly Dmitriyevich "Vitalik" Buterin. With the assistance of various co-founders, Buterin launched the original version of Ethereum in 2015. Ever since, the platform has rapidly become more and more popular and has sparked the development of new altcoins to rival bitcoin.

To acknowledge the immense potential held by Ethereum, it is necessary to comprehend the principle of a blockchain. Blockchain is the main technology behind the invention of Bitcoin in 2009. The infrastructure enables separate participants to engage with each other, without having to identify or confide with each other, and all the information regarding all the transactions is publicly stored and can be verified by anybody with an internet connection. Blockchain expedites the true power of cryptocurrencies - decentralization.

Ethereum is much more than just a peer-to-peer platform to transfer value. Unlike Bitcoin, Ethereum facilitates developers to build decentralized applications (dapps) on top of the blockchain. The platform is open source and anybody from anywhere in the world can build on Ethereum. Take the ecosystem like an app store without a central body, and lacks approval procedure to launch and run dapps. Besides, unlike centralized platforms, it does not collect any percentage of the developer's earnings for hosting dapps.

Another nifty property of the Ethereum blockchain is its ability to create and run smart contracts. A smart contract can refer to a self-executing agreement between two parties in the form of a computer code. Smart contracts can only execute if the underlying conditions are fully met. And because they are capable of eliminating the management burden, smart contracts are among the more appealing features associated with Ethereum. One can imagine a full spectrum of legal and financial contracts automated using Ethereum's smart contracts. Intrinsically, the market potential for Ethereum is monstrous.

What drives Ethereum?

Now that you understand the concept behind Ethereum, what drives Ethereum's daily price action?

There are basically four different categories that make up the Ethereum ecosystem and each of them influences the daily price. These categories include traders, investors, developers, and the end-users of different dapps hosted by the Ethereum network. Speculative traders are mainly responsible for price fluctuations because they repeatedly trade in and out of positions, often using leverage. On the other hand, investors are the staunch long-term adepts in the technology, and they hold Ethereum tokens for a prolonged period which can last up to several years. Investors have a propensity to steady prices, regularly adding to their stockpile during dips. For example, during the September 2020 sell-off, the leading 100 Ethereum addresses expanded by over 850,000 ETH tokens according to Cointelegraph consulting.

Developers and dapp users require Ethereum tokens to cater for gas fees to access the Ethereum network. To refresh your mind, gas fees refer to payments made by users to pay for computational energy needed to process and sanction transactions on the Ethereum network. As dapps and users continue to increase in number, so does the demand for Ethereum tokens.

Taking a deeper look into the Ethereum ecosystem, State of the Dapps data reveals that there are currently 2,778 total decentralized applications hosted on the Ethereum network. The number of daily active users stands at 82,660. Hiked gas prices on the Ethereum network have driven developers to seek alternative platforms with low gas fees such as the Binance Smart Chain.

Other notable factors that drive the value of ETH include:

1. Wider adoption
2. Increased acceptance
3. Government regulation
4. Mainstream media coverage
5. Market manipulation where traders buy and sell in vast quantities to influence price movement.

THREE MAIN THINGS YOU NEED TO HAVE

If you are vested in investing in Ethereum specifically, there are three main things you need to have namely:

1. An exchange account
2. A broker account and,
3. A wallet.

Exchange account

To invest in Ethereum, you need to have an exchange account. As mentioned in the previous chapter, an exchange is a digital marketplace that facilitates the buying and selling of cryptocurrencies. Picking the best exchange platform can be tiresome due to the many exchange platforms on the internet today. Here are some key factors to guide you into choosing the best exchange to buy Ethereum:

1. **Security and reliability**: Security is the main concern to many cryptocurrency traders. It is important to scrutinize the security level of an exchange platform before joining. Some exchanges are pretty bad at protecting their clients' assets due to poor security measures.

2. **Payment methods supported:** Payment methods vary from one exchange to another. Make

sure you are satisfied with the payment methods supported and before registration.

3. **Fees and commission:** Transaction fees and commission charged per trade varies with different exchange platforms. Some platforms may charge very high fees which may negatively impact the profit margin or extend a loss.

4. **User interface:** New traders prefer easy-to-operate crypto exchange platforms that do not have a lot of complex features. Trading on a complex platform with advanced tools for professional traders may result in the loss of capital.

Some other key factors that you should watch out for include geo-restrictions, liquidity, privacy policy among other factors. It would be helpful if you seek advice on which cryptocurrency exchange platform to join from a professional trader. These experienced traders can help you avoid many mistakes as you learn the trade. Now let's have a look at the best Ethereum exchange platforms that we highly recommend to new traders:

1. Coinbase

Coinbase became the first crypto-related business to be established in the United States in June 2020. Coinbase is a digital marketplace that facilitates the buying and selling of

Ethereum and more than 20 other cryptocurrencies. Besides, you can use Coinbase to swap from one cryptocurrency to another, or to send crypto to various addresses.

It is quite easy to get started on Coinbase but you must submit some personal details such as name, home address, birth date, and some other necessary information. These requirements are needed to comply with the federal laws and regulations. To buy Ethereum on Coinbase, you'll have to download the mobile app on Playstore for Android, and Apple Store for iOS. Open the app and click on get started. Register for a Coinbase account with your email address, and now you can verify your account and enter the required KYC details.

After successful account creation and verification, you can now finally proceed to buy Ethereum. On the top part of the screen, you can view a list of cryptocurrencies that you can buy on the platform. Select Ethereum and choose the amount you want to purchase. Then proceed to preview buy, and after reviewing the order you can press 'buy now.'

Why Coinbase?

- Low exchange rates
- Safe and secure
- Supports buying using fiat currency

2. Kraken

Kraken is among the earliest crypto exchange platforms to be established and supports the trading of more than 70 different cryptocurrencies including Ethereum. Kraken users enjoy several benefits including improved security, legal compliance, limit orders, and stop orders plus over 50 trading pairs to select from. The platform has many users and boasts massive trading volumes which makes it very liquid.

Why Kraken?

- Massive liquidity
- You can trade Ethereum against more than ten other cryptocurrencies
- Low transaction fees
- Kraken is available in over 90 nations

3. Bittrex

Bittrex is considered as one of the most secure crypto exchanges. The Nevada-based exchange was founded in 2014 by a team of professional traders with a combined experience of over 50 years. Bittrex supports the trading of nearly 200 different cryptocurrencies despite adopting a theme of listing only secure digital assets.

Why Bittrex?

- Low transaction fees
- Solid security
- Lists only trustworthy crypto assets
- Boasts almost 200 supported coins

Ethereum wallet

There are many Ethereum wallets circulating in the market currently. Selecting the right wallet for your Ethereum tokens will come down to a few other factors namely:

- Type of storage you will need
- Do you transact frequently?
- The platform you intend to access the wallet from (desktop, smartphone, web, etc.)

Types of Ethereum wallets

There are a number of ways that you can store your Ethereum private keys ranging from extremely secure to easily accessible methods. It is advisable to choose the method that works for you best from the different types of wallets listed below:

- **Software wallets:** Easily accessible and cheap to obtain. Best for people who transact regularly.
- **Hardware wallets:** Used to store Ethereum offline using physical chips. Examples include Ledger Nano.
- **Paper wallets:** These are papers with private keys printed on them.

Ethereum hot wallet

A hot wallet refers to a wallet that requires internet connection. Ether tokens stored in a hot wallet are easily accessible from any place on the globe. Apart from being convenient, hot wallets are not the safest out there and they can be breached by malicious actors if they obtain your login details. They are free of charge and anyone can access them from anywhere in the world. Some of the best Ethereum wallets include:

- Metamask
- Exodus
- Trust Wallet
- Mist

Ethereum cold wallet

These are physical devices used to store Ethereum offline. One of the key benefits provided of using cold wallets is the security. They are offline hence they are not susceptible to hackers. However, cold wallets tend to be expensive compared to hot wallets which are free of charge. Besides, they also support a few number of assets compared to hot wallets. Some of the best cold wallets in the market include:

- Ledger Nano
- Trezor

Ethereum broker

An Ethereum broker can be described as a digital platform that functions as a middleman between buyers and sellers in the market. There are two major types of Ethereum brokers: uncomplicated platforms that the buying and selling of ETH tokens at a fixed price, and the more sophisticated platforms that allow traders to buy and sell digital assets in real-time at the prevailing market price.

The key function of a broker is to essentially match buyers and sellers in the market. For instance, if you have a certain amount of cash and you want to buy ETH tokens, the broker finds a seller willing to sell at the price and complete the transaction. In some cases, the broker acts as both the buyer and the seller depending on the trading platform.

Complex brokerage platforms employ the concept of CFD (contract for difference) trading. Trading ETH CFDs allows you to open and close instantly and apply leveraged trading. However, it's worth noting that when you trade ETH CFDs, you don't actually own the actual Ethereum tokens but speculating on the underlying value of Ethereum as it swings.

What is the difference between an exchange and a broker?

An Ethereum broker and an Ethereum exchange are confusing to most people especially after the incorporation of broker features such as margin trading. The key difference between the two is how they operate. An Ethereum broker defines the price and commissions they are willing to sell Ethereum. They can either be the holders of the ETH tokens, or they have partnered with other platforms or brokers to ensure there is sufficient supply.

On the other hand, an Ethereum exchange involves many traders simultaneously buying and selling Ethereum pairs at the prevailing market price. However, an order is not complete until the seller agrees to the transaction.

Both brokerages and exchange platforms have existed in the traditional financial system. Ethereum's price on these exchanges is determined by the interplay between supply and demand in the market.

HOW TO TRADE ETHEREUM

Those with basic knowledge about trading can develop their strategies to trade Ethereum. It is quite easy to trade Ethereum on exchange platforms. Here is a step-by-step guide on how you can purchase ETH tokens using a fiat currency:

1. Open an account on an exchange platform

Select one exchange platform that works for your trading needs. There are very many good crypto exchange platforms out there where you can directly purchase Ethereum, unlike other smaller altcoins where you need to purchase Bitcoin first and then convert it.

After signing up, many exchange platforms will require you to submit KYC details to comply with regulatory requirements. You might be asked to submit identification proof, and proof of residence. However, there are a handful of exchanges that don't require all these details such as Changelly and Shapeshift.

2. Depositing funds

Afterward, you can fund your new account using any of the supported methods such as using a credit/debit card, bank transfer or any other method. Using credit cards is highly recommended because they are more convenient and faster. Bank transfers could take up to 5 business days to reflect in your account.

After loading your account with funds, you can now proceed and purchase Ethereum tokens.

Ethereum trading strategies

There are two major strategies for trading Ethereum. Namely:

1. Holding or 'HODLING'
2. Active trading

Buy and Hodl

As discussed earlier, Ethereum has a lot of upside potential and many investors have opted to purchase as many Ethereum tokens as possible and hold them for the long term. Long-term cryptocurrency holders require digital or hardware wallets to store their wealth. After purchasing Ethereum from an exchange, you can now transfer them to an external wallet for safekeeping since exchange platforms are not entirely secure.

Hardware wallets are the safest for long-term Ethereum holders. A hardware wallet like Trezor or Ledger Nano are highly recommended for investors who are willing to adopt this strategy. They are not susceptible to online hackers but they can be damaged or even lost.

Active/speculative trading

This trading strategy is a bit complex and requires traders to have trading basics. Different traders have different approaches when it comes to speculating on the future price of Ethereum namely:

1. Day trading

Ethereum's massive popularity means it has a high trading volume and liquidity. Ethereum day traders rely on the volatile Ethereum market and speculate on short-term price swings. They capitalize on short-term price movements to gain profits and close all their positions before the end of the day.

2. Swing trading

This ETH trading approach involves generating profits from "swinging' Ether price. This is one of the most popular trading methods in all financial markets including stocks, forex, and crypto. Ethereum swingers tend to hold on to a position for a number of days extending up to weeks before selling. Swing trading is ideal for trading Ethereum because its value can rise or fall within short periods of time.

ETHEREUM TRADING COMES WITH RISKS

The initial step to proper risk management is to learn the risks associated with trading Ethereum, their likelihood, and their intensity. Risks can come from different sources and they come in different ways. Below we have analyzed some of the common risks associated with Ethereum:

1. Regulatory risks

More than a decade after the introduction of the pioneering cryptocurrency, regulating it has remained to be quite a challenge in most nations. Authorities are confused whether cryptocurrencies like Bitcoin and Ethereum are assets, commodities, a means of payment, or financial instruments. Also, on the case of the Ethereum network, authorities could clamp down IPOs or crowd shares affecting development on the network.

2. Competitive risk

One of the biggest risks facing Ethereum is the possibility of a faster and more efficient rival coming up and replacing it.

Given the project's code is open-source, the possibility of this happening is very high. Binance smart chain has emerged to be a formidable rival to the Ethereum network due to Ethereum's hiked gas fees. Some developers have opted to migrate to more efficient and affordable platforms such as Binance smart chain.

3. Technical risks

The blockchain sharding and scaling is not 100 percent guaranteed to work. Loopholes on the code might be discovered in the future. Ethereum's transition to 2.0 might flop affecting the market.

4. Malleability

Another major risk facing the Ethereum network is the malleability of its code in contrast to Bitcoin. Given the development of the Ethereum network over the years, it would be difficult to enhance meaningful adjustments to its functionality.

TWO TIPS FOR BEGINNERS ON ETHEREUM TRADING

1. Use both technical and fundamental analysis

To improve your accuracy in speculating future price movements of Ether, you should learn how to conduct technical analysis to identify market trends and movements. Most popular trading platforms provide users with a variety of tools and indicators to use in technical analysis.

On the other hand, Ethereum is underpinned by the robust blockchain technology. As such, its development and growth depend on many other factors including blockchain activity, changes made by the developers, public sentiment on Ethereum, and launch of new products on the platform. For this reason, as a new trader you should always keep an eye on the fundamental factors that may drive or dip the price of Ethereum.

2. Risk management is important

Even though Ethereum has a very big upside potential, it is a massively volatile cryptocurrency. As such, it is vital for new traders to instill discipline and learn risk management skills to avoid making unnecessary losses. It would be helpful for a beginner to start small and add their capital as they gain more experience in the crypto trading landscape. As you gain more confidence and skills, you can start using leverage and stake more funds.

ARE ALTCOINS BETTER?

GETTING INTO ALTCOINS

What are Altcoins? Are they still part of the cryptocurrency world? Are they better than Bitcoin? Let us find out. These questions pop up in the minds of everyone trying to trade cryptocurrencies other than Bitcoin. Now, we get that Bitcoin is dominative and as popular as anyone can imagine. Everyone has probably heard of it. However, Altcoins, or alternative coins, are simply any other cryptocurrency apart from Bitcoin. There are 2,000+ alternative coins that one can choose from, but none is as renowned as Bitcoin.

Different altcoins with some Bitcoin features emerge day after day with the ultimate goal of replacing Bitcoin and the traditional financial system at some point in their lifespan.

Experts argue that most altcoins are primarily cloning Bitcoins, given their insignificant attempt to change their transaction speed and algorithms. Some experts disregard the existence of altcoins since some do not endure in the crypto market. However, altcoins have proven to be vital in the quest to achieve decentralization.

Furthermore, without altcoins, Bitcoin would enjoy a monopoly in the crypto market. Most people may not realize it now, but altcoins provide the necessary competition that the market requires. They also encourage developers to continue innovating and coming up with outstanding characteristics that assist in furthering decentralization.

Why People Should Adopt Altcoins

Like bitcoins, people can make money using altcoins. However, the deal of altcoins is not entirely to make money. In this sense, there are several reasons why people should start embracing altcoins. These include:

- **The future of finance is cryptocurrency –** Imagine transacting or making payments without worrying about your privacy, identity, and security. This is what cryptocurrency promises to bring to the table in this technological era where data is stolen or sold by corporates. In the middle of it all are the altcoins.

- **Altcoins have unbelievable returns** – But well, you have to believe that you can gain 100% or 1000% returns daily or monthly, respectively. However, these can only be achieved with vast knowledge of the trade.

- **Altcoins are currently on the rise** – Thanks to the publicity Bitcoin has gained. With time, people will give altcoins the same attention they have given Bitcoin.

- **One does not require a lot of money to start trading** – One can begin trading with as low as one can afford and still manage to make huge returns. Credits to the power of compound interest!

Altcoins Vs. Bitcoin and Ethereum

There is very little difference between Bitcoin and alternative coins. However, the principal argument that has separated the fight between altcoins and Ethereum and Bitcoin has been based on the ability to transact instantly when using altcoins. This has enabled trade between merchants and their customers without worrying about the legitimacy of the payments since the payment is reflected immediately.

Besides, Bitcoin differs from altcoins in the fluctuation rate and their creation schedule. Altcoins mainly attract investors by their different unique characteristics, and other altcoins emerge or are created day in day out. Economists, however, argue that a stable currency is more desirable compared to one prone to inflation.

Another argument is based on the Proof-of-Stake. All altcoins do is supplement or replace the Proof-of-Stake scheme that Bitcoin uses. Thereby, altcoins show great growth potential. Moreover, altcoins thrive at adding functionalities that are not available on, or not possible to experience with, Bitcoin.

Pros of Trading Altcoins

Trading in altcoins has its benefits. A trader can place their trade in their respective locality or even home and still manage to garner profits for a start. Furthermore, a trader can reap huge returns/profits quickly from trading altcoins compared to Bitcoin. The transaction is also instant.

Pump and dump traders can hike the prices of their assets freely in a process called "pump". The pumped assets are actually of lesser costs. The traders can sell or dump their assets when the prices of the assets are at their peak. Again, volatility acts as an advantage to the traders because a trader may win big just as much as he/she may lose big.

Cons of Trading Altcoins

Altcoin trading has its downsides too. For instance, the instability or volatility that has been considered an advantage can still harm a trader as it may cause a trader enormous losses. Subsequently, most trading platforms do not allow the withdrawal of fiat. The trader is therefore pushed to convert altcoins to Bitcoin before they can withdraw. The transaction fees involved in the conversion may be discouraging.

WHAT DO YOU NEED?

Great question! The first instinct of every trader is to make profits by making sales. However, trading altcoins does not begin and end with having money in your pocket and a passion for the trade. The trader will need the following in his/her corner:

1. Trading Basics

Learning the basics of trading is the preliminary step into any trading, and trading altcoins is no different. First, the aspiring trader must understand the market. Knowledge is power. Knowing what you are diving into is the first step towards becoming a successful trader. It gives you an insight when choosing the assets you want to invest in.

The trader has to learn the market's movements to know when to enter and exit the market, i.e., when to hold onto an asset and when to make a sale. Selling investments at the appropriate time is just as essential as knowledge of when to buy them. Initial Coin Offerings (ICOs) often tend to excite starters. The ICOs blind newbies by the little profits first offer guarantees. The trick that ICOs play people is the promise of returns on their tokens with time, and people fall for them. It is advisable to do extensive research on new tokens before making investments in them. This knowledge enables the trader to come up with a strategy that works for them.

2. Strategy

Picking the strategy that works to achieve your objective makes trading a lot easier. The strategy you choose is also dependent on the vendor you will choose. Vendors with a solid technical team create more chances of meeting your goals. A strategy is a plan on how to go about trading, when, and where the trade happens.

You will also require a goal to work towards so that your strategy gives you the compass towards meeting these set goals. Sticking to the plan instills discipline in a trader to know their limits.

3. A Good and Trustworthy Broker

Another hassle that an altcoin trader will most definitely face is finding the right broker, especially with scammers and frauds on the loose. Different brokers have different features, including the lists of altcoins, fiat money support, or support Bitcoin/altcoin deposit. Your choice should contain elements that are vital for and convenience your trading. What are the pairing cryptos? What are the broker's trading fees? What is the background of the broker? Some of the best Altcoin brokers include Binance, Bitmax, Bittrex, Crex24, Bitfinex, and many more. A review of their features won't hurt.

4. An altcoin to trade

The choice of the best altcoin to trade is half the trading battle. Much emphasis is customarily placed on liquidity and volatility. Most traders go for altcoins with high volatility and high liquidity. High volatility means that traders stand a chance for higher returns on their investments but also more significant losses. However, it is a risk worth taking. High liquidity necessitates a trader to lend to and borrow from a liquidity pool with much ease.

Other factors to consider when choosing an altcoin include its legality. Some coins are banned in some countries, thus it is wise to own an altcoin asset that is legal in one's nation.

5. Trading Platform

Where do you buy and sell altcoins? Finding the best trading platform for altcoin exchange can prove to be a hassle sometimes. There are hundreds of platforms that offer crypto wallets, but each comes with its benefits and disadvantages. It is the initiative of the trader to review their fees, availability, trading volume, security measures, and usability. This way, the trader is able to choose the best altcoin exchange platform that works seamlessly with his/her trading strategy.

On the contrary, some platforms allow crypto-to-crypto exchange while some don't. Interoperability is essential in altcoins since you will be required to convert altcoins into bitcoins before withdrawing. Furthermore, owning a crypto wallet in a platform that allows maximum trading volume and pairs pronounces that transactions are super-fast regardless of the time and amount.

The right platform should enable customer support that will assist when the trader encounters a problem. It should also be user-friendly with suitable analytical tools that make trading fun for the trader while minimizing trading risks. So, where can you buy and sell altcoins?

What You Need?

Most alternative coins are not here to stay and should not be perceived as a long-term investment. It is also a risky game, more of a gamble, where you can win or lose. Hence, having this information will assist in making the right decision that will lead to your gain.

Consequently, having the appropriate knowledge will allow you to place your investments in solid technologies. Solid technologies will eliminate the risk of coins disappearing from the market for the trader. The trader will also gain knowledge of how to manage and mitigate other dangers that he/she may encounter.

START TRADING WITH ALTCOINS

Having come to the conclusion that altcoins can and will work for you, you will have to decide whether to use decentralized or centralized exchanges. The decision on which exchange to pick will depend on the metrics that favored your choice. Some of these metrics are; convenience, security, decentralization and price levels, liquidity, and commission fees. The step of choosing the method of exchange is just as important as finding the right altcoin.

Trading altcoins involves the following procedure:

Step 1: Sign up to a trading Platform

Register for an altcoin exchange account with a cryptocurrency platform of your choice.

Step 2: Set up an altcoin wallet

Having an altcoin wallet enables you to deposit crypto assets and trade them. There are three different types of altcoin wallets to choose from. Your choice may be mobile wallet app, hardware, or software wallets.

Mobile wallet app is designed for mobile phone usage only. It is more preferred due to added security provided you have a strong password and for its mobility. On the other hand, the hardware wallet stores private keys and are free from virus attacks. Losing the private keys means that you will also lose the altcoins in your wallet. Hardware wallets are the safest way to store tokens since the access key is not transferred from the wallet. They are, however, very costly. Software wallets are prone to viruses and other malicious attacks, but they are free and flexible. The choice of wallet is all in your hands.

Step 3: Find crypto wallet address.

Finding an altcoin wallet address is simply choosing the right coin for trade from the list of alternative coins. Clicking on the deposit button generates the wallet address.

Step 4: Deposit into your wallet address

Send money from your account to the wallet address generated. Getting the correct wallet address is mandatory since transferring to the wrong address results in losing the investment. Wait for a moment for the deposit to reflect on your trading platform account.

Step 5: Start trading.

You can finally choose which altcoin to buy or sell with the crypto deposited into your account.

If you intend to trade altcoins on Binance, you have to create a Binance trading account and secure it with a strong password. Then enable two-factor authentication to notify you when someone attempts accessing your account. You can then deposit money in your account in the "Deposits/Withdrawal" section. The process generates an address that will receive altcoins from your wallet. With the funds in your account, you can finally trade on the "Exchange" section.

ALTCOIN DAY TRADING RISKS

Day trading has potential rewards like high returns for the right altcoin and market research. Taking high risks gives a 50-50 chance to a trader, high risk-return tradeoffs of significant loss. These potential rewards of day trading altcoins come with several risks. Understanding the risks involved places a trader in an excellent position to know how to evade or mitigate them. Some of the risks involved include:

i. High volatility – Altcoins are known for being hugely volatile. The volatility is usually dictated by supply and demand. The rising and falling of prices are autonomous of real-world assets; thus, fluctuation is short-term. The ability to die makes it a threat even for day traders. It is also possible to lose gains when this fluctuation happens to a trader holding on to long-term altcoins.

ii. Susceptible to manipulation of prices – Remember pump-and-dump? The prices of assets can be hiked depending on the preference of the asset holders. Small inflow and outflow of capitalization and low trade volumes also significantly affect the market prices.

iii. Prone to value loss – The woe of a day trader is the value of altcoins drastically dropping when their unique technology or features becomes outdated. This is amongst the reasons most altcoins become obsolete as quickly as they are created.

iv. Regulation issues – Governments and regulatory bodies make the taxes and rules unpredictable, given that most altcoins are not legal in some nations. Regulations also make altcoins less and less interesting.

v. Crypto-fraud and swindle susceptibility – Due to bans in some regions and lack of regulation of altcoins, scammers and fraudsters find it easier to trick and manipulate traders. An instance happened with OneCoin that sold nonexistent cryptocurrencies, and its founder disappeared with over $4 billion worth of people's investments.

vi. Consumer protection – Altcoins, and bitcoin too, do not have collateral as a way of safeguarding investments.

vii. High risk – The volatility of altcoins make them extremely risky even for day trading.

ALTCOIN TRADING RISK MITIGATION

Crypto trading is luxurious if the losses are considerable and the wins big. Making this realistic requires doing the trading right. However, one cannot be too careful when chasing after high returns. To avoid making the same mistakes, risk mitigation and management is necessary. Some of these mitigation measures include:

Making small investments and slow moves – the fear of missing out overwhelms traders into making last-minute trades when the market is at its peak. The trend tends to reverse abruptly, and the trader stands to lose. At this point, it is essential to recall that patience is a virtue. Learn about the market, altcoin risks, and make small trades and progress upwards slowly until you achieve your goals. In summary, it is inadvisable to invest a massive amount of your deposits on a single altcoin. In addition, do not invest more than 50% of the deposit on long-term altcoins.

Set stop-loss – This is a good way of fixing profits and managing losses by cutting out duds. A trader should close trading when the profit target has been achieved by positioning the size and average down.

Position sizing trades – Never go all in lest you intend to lose all your deposit. You won't last long this way.

Don't purchase during an altcoin's peak moments – When altcoins are gaining popularity, beginners are typically tempted to deep-dive into it, thus purchasing them. On the contrary, they should buy fiat when the prices are high. The prices are prone to drastically drop or go back to the original prices; thus, the trader may incur huge losses.

Purchase coins at the bottom – This guarantees winning positions if the trader will not be greedy when selling. It is more desirable to have numerous small profits than having to await huge gains from a single holding position.

Diverse selling order – Having diverse selling order and hard profits acts as insurance of maximum reward. In the event of maximum gains, it is crucial to lock in some gains, that is, withdrawing from your crypto wallets.

Always have a strategy – always have a game plan when trading altcoins and stick to it. The plan is what separates gamblers from pro traders. The gambler relies on possibilities while the pro trader relies on probabilities. The pro trader, however, prepares for both possibility and probability.

THREE TIPS ON ALTCOIN TRADING

To get the most out of day trading altcoins, you will need some tips to get you started. First, the novelty of crypto day trading should tell you that you need to **be alert**. Stay updated with crypto news and market movements. Pulling day trading off requires vigilance. Since Bitcoin movements have an effect on the prices of altcoins, you need to keep an eye on Bitcoin. Positive Bitcoin news has a significant impact on the rest of the cryptocurrencies. While keeping your focus on Bitcoin, also beware of the changes altcoins make independent of Bitcoin.

Despite the hype on altcoins, Bitcoin always has a way of finding its way into the story. Therefore, **do not ignore Bitcoin.** Matter-of-factly, it is the best performing cryptocurrency, and it would be stupid to ignore it. Your goal of trading in altcoins is not to avoid Bitcoin but to make profits. Bitcoin also serves a similar purpose. Know when to make this choice.

Learn. Learn. Learn. And keep learning. Learn how to use hot and cold wallets. Do not trust a single source, but do extensive research on altcoins and learn more about the market caps. The cryptocurrency concept is still new, and new technologies and features keep popping up. It is difficult to say that one is entirely conversant with altcoins. Have an eye for recent trends and the gist to be knowledgeable.

11

DAY TRADING STRATEGIES

DAY TRADING EXPLAINED

Day trading is more suitable for short-term trading that relies on small and frequent market movements. The intraday trader holds crypto assets for a few seconds or hours and sells them at a higher price. The main idea of day trading strategies is to try to maximize returns based on market volatility. Hence, the trader opens and closes positions during the day but does not generally hold any positions overnight. A day trader requires an apt understanding of the market.

The ultimate goal of day trading strategies is to create more winning positions than losing positions. Some systems generate more losing positions than winning positions. However, the most important aspects are the average wins and the net results that involve more significant risks to achieve the potential profits. If the average wins are more than the average loss or the net results produced are positive, then the strategy serves its purpose. Some of the techniques covered in this chapter include Scalping, HFT, and Range Trading.

Factors to Consider

What does day trading rely on? Two factors have an effect on the market and the assets. In return, day trading strategy is affected. These factors are:

Volatility – This refers to how frequently the price of an asset changes. An asset whose value changes often is very volatile. A non-volatile asset, on the other hand, retains its market value for a very long time.

Liquidity – Liquidity is simply how easy you can purchase an asset and how easy it is to sell it. If the asset can be sold quickly, it is regarded as very liquid, and vice-versa.

Importance of Having a Strategy

- **Allows a trader to measure their performance** – A good trading strategy leaves room for a trader to assess and evaluate their performance, giving them a basis to improve. The strategy also allows the trader to develop a statistical database of their strategy that assists in comparing trading history and current results. Thus, a trader can change several bedrock parameters to oversee the success in the failed areas.

- **Enables a trader to maintain focus** – Having a predetermined day trading strategy instills discipline into trading activities. Therefore, a trader is not easily distracted by the inflow of trading news that may impede their analysis process.

- **Assists in keeping the trader's trading limits in check** – It is easy to get over-ambitious about positions, especially with the influence of professional traders or friends. A strategy with transparent entry signals and exit rules helps a trader stick to his/her lane to avoid overtrading. The trader, thus, ends up with a net positive expectancy.

- **Aids management of emotions** – One of the critical tricks to becoming a successful day trader is ruling out one's feelings during staking. Greed, for instance, may often lead to bad trades when the trader realizes that he/she is on a winning streak if they open more positions or stake more cash. Fear of losing, on the contrary, deters a trader from entering a good position or stakes less money.

- **Helps in money management** – A solid trading strategy assists in making money decisions like withdrawal and deposit amounts, funds to invest, and the trading fees.

Finding the right trading strategy is the key to successful day trading. The plan should be simple, tried, tested, and approved. However practical and successful an approach is, strategies are subject to drawdowns and bound to become obsolete at some point. Hence, they should constantly be monitored for fine-tuning when their performance begins to deteriorate.

HAVE YOU HEARD OF SCALPING?

If you are into entering and exiting markets as quickly as possible while placing multiple trades on the same day, then scalping is meant for you. The scalper is a day trader that prioritizes high trade volumes against small market price changes for several little profits. The scalper's goal is not to make huge profits in a single investment. This aspect makes day trading more manageable even under duress; thus, it is a less risky strategy. It is also a relatively straightforward concept. There are two types of scalpers, a discretionary scalper, and a systematic scalp trader. The discretionary places trade as the market unfolds, relying on gut feeling and intuition. On the other hand, a systematic scalper has a well-defined policy with specific entry and exit points.

For scalping to be an effective strategy, the trader has to have a strict exit rule. One significant loss could mean losing all the small profits that added up from the previous deals. This style of trading requires discipline, quick decision-making, and stamina from the trader. They are required to make a decision based on charts within 1-5 minute intervals. Therefore, a scalper needs to know how to study and interpret short-term graphs and charts.

Scalping requires that one stays alert for high volatile assets, that is, investments with positive trends, and anticipate upswings and downswings. The scalper then buys these assets, sells the asset upswing, and makes profits several times a day. They use stop-losses and leverage. Why scalping though? Scalping aids in evading pitfalls of poorly timing the peak moments and overexposure and failing to make any profits.

How it Works as a Trading Strategy

How exactly is scalping done, and how do scalpers make money? The scalper finds a high volatile liquid asset with future price changes throughout the day, buys the asset at a lower price, and sells it at a small profit. He/she then creates another opportunity before the market falls.

Scalping works on the following premises:

- Small movements are easier to get
- Limiting risks by fewer exposures
- Frequent small moves

Scalping relies on technical analysis – the history of price changes and the trends that caused the changes. The scalper uses some tools and charts to study patterns for the prediction of price movements. If the signal is positive, the trader buys the asset for resale. Timeframes used in the analysis may be five seconds, but the scalper can make a hundred trades from it. The factors that make this strategy a success include support and resistance levels, trade volumes, chart patterns, price action, etc.

Pros and Cons

Scalping aims to identify small market movements within the shortest time possible. Scalping thus requires discipline and wit. Its advantages include:

- **Limited exposure to the market** – scalpers are only vulnerable to market changes for a short time.

- **Profit from a slow market** - a strict exit strategy brings pure profits to the scalper. They can leverage small price changes that may not appear on the overall trend.
- **Not being stuck in a reversal** - scalping is non-directional, meaning that it can take advantage regardless of the market's direction. Scalpers can get out when the asset starts declining and still make profits.
- **Creates more winning positions** – scalping reduces the losses using leverage and tight stop-losses, making the winning rate around 80 percent in the multiple trades.
- **Requires minimum trading capital** – small profits are gained consecutively since a trader does not require waiting for long to realize profits.
- Since scalping is based on technical criteria, scalping strategies are easily automated within a trading system.

Its disadvantages include:

- **Missing out on the big wins** - it relies on making the most trades to make reasonable profits. The risk of making small profits on multiple trades is not worth the effort sometimes compared to holding winning positions for long.

- **Difficulty in making predictions** –
  Predicting consistent, correct outcomes on a short-term basis is quite the task. Part of the prediction requires entering and exiting the market at the right positions.

- **Psychological exhaustion** - It is time-consuming and needs a high concentration level. Waiting for the right positions to enter markets could mean 'no bathroom' breaks.

- **Commissions piling up** - maximum trades mean that the transaction costs are also higher since each trade requires that a commission is paid.

How to Apply Scalping

First, you need to set a target amount of profit per trade, crosscheck the asset's price in the market against the set target profit, and finally follow the trends to create a 'hot' watch list. What makes a good scalper is their ability to observe and interpret the trends and short-term charts. Apart from spotting market trends and following news, you should understand the psychology of the bull and bear market.

For scalping to work, a trader is required to have liquidity and sufficient capital and ensure they have access to live bids and a good internet connection. Too much latency could mean that the data being received is dated, hence missing the entry and exit points of a trade. To evade missing out, scalpers use Level 2 quotation for tracking of asset prices. Therefore, a trader should look for critical technical indicators like moving averages, Relative Strength Index, VWAP, Fibonacci retracement tool, and Bollinger Bands. Alternatively, they can opt to identify trade setups using trade volumes, price actions, chart patterns, etc. You can also create your indicator if using real-time order book analysis, open interest, and volume profile does not excite you.

IN RANGE OF RANGE TRADING

A range is the state of the market, especially after a trend. According to Investopedia, Range Trading refers to a given range between two price levels: low and high prices, where trade occurs only within this range. A trader continues with their trade until the asset is out of this range. The market movement has to be consistent during range trading. A trader purchases cryptocurrencies at the lower end of the spectrum and sells them at the high end over a short period.

How it works

There is a positive or negative movement of the market after a trend since prices bounce between highs and lows. We do not expect a trading range to last forever; hence, the cost of an asset may break above or fall below a trading range. These movements are called breakout and breakdown, respectively. Breakdowns and breakouts imply that traders are participating when high volumes are involved. Thus, overselling and overbuying can occur. When the high end of the range breaks, it means that an upward trend has begun. A trader should stop trading against the existing trend. Subsequently, when the lower end of the range is broken, a downtrend starts and a trader should be ready to sell short.

A trader can buy a cryptocurrency when it approaches its support level and sells towards its trendline resistance level. Support levels are the price levels with high demand from buyers and the unwillingness of sellers to sell. On the contrary, resistance occurs when the sellers are willing to sell, and buyers become unwilling to buy. Candlestick patterns are used to help spot entry points. It becomes easier to see the price retracing when approaching the resistance or support levels. Range trading requires that a trader buys at support and sells at resistance. The trader follows the candlestick pattern confirmation to place a trade in the direction of the movement.

The profit should always be more significant than the risk in range trading. The odds against the reward ratio should also be realistic. If the potential profit doubles the risk, a trader places a stop-loss under the current bullish candle when purchasing and above the current bearish candle when selling. Range trading uses volume trends, price actions, RSI, and other indicators to validate overbought and oversold conditions.

Pros and Cons

The advantages of Range Trading include:

- *Small starting funds* – Range Trade requires little capital to start.
- *Familiarity* – Range Trading is all about a range between the lows and highs; thus, a trader is familiar with the prices that might occur in-between.
- *Transparent targets and stops* – A trader can cut losses and take profits from the market within the specified range.
- *No waiting around* – Once profit is realized, a trader can opt out of the market. Staying in the market for long attracts losing the funds.

- *Non-directional* – Traders can place both buy and sell orders regardless of the market's direction and still make profits or reduce losses.

The cons of Range Trading are:

- *The cost* – Range trading involves small investments that are accompanied by transaction costs. These fees pile up to an enormous amount compared to trading strategies that include taking more significant risks.
- *Rapid decision-making* – In a tight range, a trader is required to make a quick decision on when to enter a market to maximize profits.
- *Pin-point entry points* – entering a trade in the middle of a range could result in missing out on returns. The entry and exit points are essential.

Risks Involved and Mitigation

Range Trading suffers from the following risks:

Price fluctuation – temporary price movements below support or above resistance cause temporary price fluctuations that attract investors into purchasing or selling short.

False or actual breakout – A crypto can move out of range and bounce back.

Market timing – The market timing should be precise so that the trader knows when and how long a trading range will last.

Price direction knowledge – Lack of understanding of the direction the price will move risks a trader losing their assets.

To mitigate these risks, a Range trader must exit a range should the crypto move out of range. This discipline can be achieved using stop-losses. Alternatively, they should avoid placing trades in the middle of a range and practice precision.

HFT! HIGH-FREQUENCY TRADING

Traditional markets suffer from trade volumes, time, speed, and price. To realize profits with large trade volumes, data processing at high speeds is necessary. Do you need to place orders and crypto trades faster and achieve quick results? Worry not, for High-Frequency Trading comes to your rescue. HFT is a trading strategy revolving around algorithms. It uses powerful computers and fast internet speeds to analyze news, big data, and crucial information that facilitates buying of assets quickly with utmost precision. The key aspect of HFT is the speed.

Is HFT applicable in cryptocurrencies?

Yeah. Unfortunately, not everyone can apply it. It is somewhat more suited for institutions. The fundamental principle that strengthens its applicability is colocation. Colocation relies on the proximity of a trading server to an exchange data center. The server is in the same facility as the data center; hence, it achieves low latency in data transmission. Besides colocation, it is used by arbitrageurs and crypto day traders. It opens multiple positions and conducts trades faster than a regular crypto day-trader.

How it works

The critical aspects of HFT include high speeds, collocation services, short timeframes for opening and closing positions, multiple orders submission, and evading overnight risks. HFT computers are made to host complex algorithms that analyze cryptocurrency data across all exchanges in milliseconds to achieve this automation. These algorithms detect trends and market changes that a human cannot perceive, even a professional trader.

The algorithms open several positions at high speed based on the analysis conducted by powerful computers. When large traders open a large, long, or short position, the trend sways to the direction of that trade. HFT algorithms take the opposite direction by buying the dip and exit when the prices swing back to normal. However, HFT algorithms may sometimes go against the opposite side. Besides, the main goal is to detect short-term anomalies in small price movements and benefit from them.

When is HFT Best for Use?

Since HFT depends on price changes, it is best suited for Bitcoin's volatility because it does not add volatility. According to Mondovision, the continued low volatility of Bitcoin resulted from increased HFT use in the cryptocurrency realm. Moreover, HFT solves Bitcoin's problem of liquidity since it adds liquidity. If you are looking for excellent scalability, then now is the right time to use HFT. The promoted platform also has to be 100% efficient, and the algorithm satisfies your trading needs.

Pros and Cons

Some of the merits of using HFT include:

- *Speed and automation* – traders are thrilled at the speed and automation that come with HFT. These aspects help them leverage profits by spotting market opportunities without human intervention.
- *Increases competition and levels prices* – HFT

traders compete with other HFT traders. It helps in price discovery and formation processes by bringing liquidity to the market.

- *Eliminate potential errors* – HFT is automated and precise, devoid of human errors by using complex mathematical algorithms to analyze the market trends, news, and trading processes.

The disadvantages of using HFT includes:

- *Displaces human traders from the market* – individual traders cannot compete with institutions since HFT places them at a disadvantage.
- *Finding a suitable algorithm is a hassle* – a trader may fall victim to fraud or even end up with unapproved algorithms that attract losses.

Risks Involved and How to Manage Them

Despite the increasing acceptance of High-Frequency Trading in the world of digital assets, it threatens market manipulation. Thus, conducting due diligence before going all-in should be prioritized. Some of the risks involved include:

High risk to reward ratio – Compared to traditional trading strategies, the risk-reward ratio is exceptionally high in HFTs. Positions may sometimes result in lower profits than anticipated. The loss may be significant in the event multiple opened positions result in a loss in a bid to harness more profit.

Faulty algorithms – A trader may fall victim to fraud to attract them to make advance payments and ghost them later. Otherwise, a trader's supposed algorithm of choice may not be proven to work, resulting in loss to the trader.

Potential favoritism and market manipulation – Allegedly, HFT contributed to the flash crashes, i.e., market manipulation and unnecessary volatility. Expensive HFT also gives a particular group more opportunities at the expense of small players in the market.

Room for illegal exploitation – HFT can deceive the system by placing ghost orders and immediately canceling them after triggering a short-term increase in prices.

We can mitigate these risks to make HFT work for just anyone. How?

Start small – Traders should stick to manual day trading and refine their way up strategies until they gain the adequate experience necessary for HFT.

Understand the Market – HFT involves complex algorithms that require advanced traders. Beginners should be cautious when applying HFT. It demands a certain level of expertise, thus, more suitable for institutions compared to individual traders.

Take time to find the right algorithm – Finding the suitable algorithm that works to meet your objectives places you at an advantage in the market.

CHOOSING THE BEST STRATEGY FOR YOU

A successful day trading career begins with finding the best strategy. A strategy that leads towards meeting the goals of a trader is usually the best. There is no such thing as the right strategy because what works for one trader may not work for another. Finding this strategy that works for you requires an individual to follow specific criteria in their selection. These criteria are as follows:

1. **Studying profits and losses of individual strategies** – what is the profit and loss history of a strategy? What are the potential gains of using a particular strategy? Is it worth it?
2. **Trading timeframe** – how much time are you willing to spend on a trade? Minutes? Hours? Days?
3. **Access to markets** – Some strategies may be

ruled out when using brokers that limit your leverage and hedging.

4. **Individual skillset –** a strategy is only as good as the individual. Find a strategy that is compatible with your personality and skills.

5. **Effort –** How much are you prepared to be involved in your trading?

6. **Risks against rewards –** consider risk management when selecting a strategy. You should also consider the risk-reward ratio of a system to determine the potential profits and potential losses.

7. **The complexity of the strategy –** Day trading has strategies with varying degrees of sophistication. Therefore, you should consider the complexity of a strategy before choosing to use it.

8. **Independence of a strategy –** A strategy should not be wholly dependent on indicators. Humans make indicators, and they are not usually 100 percent of the time correct.

To sum it up, a profitable day trader needs to be committed to their trading strategy and keep their emotions at bay. Day trading should be more intuitive; hence some may not find it amusing when strategies do not work. It is important to note that a single strategy cannot be expected to work on all occasions. Different approaches work on different occasions.

IV

WHAT YOU SHOULD LEARN ASIDE FROM TRADING

12

ANALYZING FUNDAMENTALLY

DO I NEED TO KNOW THIS?

Trading in the dynamic and unpredictable cryptocurrency market requires that a trader masters the necessary skills to successfully perform his/her trades. Such mastery includes practicing analysis before making investments, i.e., qualitative analysis, quantitative analysis, fundamental analysis, and technical analysis. Fundamental analysts ensure that they do not place trades blindly. Despite the complexities of analyzing crypto fundamentally, the laws of economics still apply. Therefore, the supply and demand of cryptocurrencies could be analyzed to aid crypto trading.

Who uses Fundamental analysis?

Long-term traders, value investors and equity analysts looking into a favorable pricing of a cryptocurrency or a stock usually use FA. They use this analysis to determine whether the price of a stock or crypto has a positive prospect.

IMPORTANCE OF FUNDAMENTAL ANALYSIS

Is fundamental analysis important? Do you need it? Why? The whole idea of fundamental analysis is finding the value of an asset.

The following ways portray how beneficial fundamental analysis is to you as a trader.

1. Management evaluation

A company is as good as its management. And so is a blockchain network. Fundamental analysis helps a trader understand the structure of the management and how efficient it is. FA also assists in defining the past performance of a company.

2. Analyzing the strength of a crypto or stock

The most important aspect to look at in a company is its financial strength regardless of how good the management is. Analyzing fundamentally ensures that the financial performance of an asset is carefully scrutinized without predetermined parameters.

3. Determine the competitiveness of an asset

What competitive advantage does an asset have over its peers? The ability of an asset to outperform its competitors is determined by the financial performance. If the performance is good, then it has a better chance of competing in the market. Otherwise, its extinction is imminent. Fundamental analysis helps determine this.

4. Determine an intrinsic value

FA analyzes an asset's performance history to come up with a fair value for the asset. Thus, it is easy to determine whether an asset is undervalued or overvalued. An asset is said to be undervalued if the current market price is lower than the intrinsic or value. Such careful analysis helps a trader in choosing the right cryptocurrency to invest in.

5. Prediction of market price movement

One of the challenges long-term investors face when investing in crypto is determining the correct future price of crypto. This is mostly influenced by the volatility of cryptocurrencies. One moment the price may be experiencing an uptrend then the next it crumbles down.

Fundamental analysis comes in handy when studying the economy and the industry to forecast price movements.

Therefore, a crypto trader can use fundamental analysis in identifying the asset with the highest potential to grow. Thus, on-setting huge returns. If you intend to gain from long-term trading, it is wise to learn fundamental analysis to determine the safety of your investment in the long run. Such knowledge will assist you in identifying an asset with a strong financial performance, hence, a surety of its longevity in the market.

WHAT IS FUNDAMENTAL ANALYSIS

Fundamental analysis is defined as a method used by investors and traders in determining an asset's fair value. Despite the numerous approaches of establishing the value of a crypto, fundamental analysis proves to be the most integral for determining its true value. Therefore, the main focus of FA is the performance metrics of an asset.

FA is used to identify undervalued or overvalued assets in the market based on their fair market value. It works on the assumption that investors will be attracted to lower prices so that they can sell at higher prices. That is, when the asset is underpriced, an investor will buy, and when it is overvalued, an investor will sell.

How it Works

Fundamental analysis works on the assumption that the market price of an asset may be incorrectly quoted in the short run, but the market still works to correct the wrong value. It takes understanding where the crypto derives its value to conduct FA. FA looks at the underlying internal and external factors that could possibly influence the price of an asset. After identifying strong crypto metrics, FA deep dives into the available information. How many people are using it? What are the use cases of the asset in question? An investor looks at the economic environment of the crypto, political influence, the team behind its network, its competitiveness in the market, its intrinsic value, etc.

Because a single measure cannot be used to determine the value of an asset, FA uses on-chain metrics, project metrics, financial metrics amongst other measures. In on-chain metrics, the analyst studies the data on the blockchain network by simply pulling the information from related APIs. The information may be the number of transactions, the trading fees, transaction value, etc. The project metrics, on the other hand, look at the qualitative data of the team's performance, the whitepaper, and a prospective roadmap. The financial metrics covers the information about the trade volume, liquidity, market cap, and many more.

Goals of Using FA

What objectives are achieved by using fundamental analysis? The main goal of using fundamental analysis is to establish whether an asset is undervalued or overvalued. This information gives investors the knowledge of when to enter and exit a market position.

Other objectives include:

- To evaluate an asset and determine if its price will rise or fall.
- To project the performance of an asset.
- To estimate the risks related to the asset.
- To evaluate the management of the asset and its financial constraints.
- To determine the fair value (intrinsic value) of the asset.

Why you should use FA

Doing fundamental analysis correctly provides insight for investors to separate an asset's market value from its true market cap. Other approaches may give you results, but the data obtained may not always tell you why those results were achieved.

Alternatively, investors may view the market movements based on their personal beliefs, culture, or professional backgrounds. Using FA allows you to use your own perspective to predict the market movements. However, it is advisable to incorporate technical analysis with your fundamental analysis to find where the price will pick or fall.

THE PROS AND CONS OF FA

Fundamental analysis is not exclusively beneficial. This means that it has its merits and demerits. Its advantages include:

- **Gives a comprehensive outlook** – FA considers specific factors that are related to the economy and crypto industry. Thus, giving it a comprehensive perspective.
- **Ideal for long-term traders** – It is used to determine the true value of an asset based on long-term trends making it suitable for establishing long-term results.
- **Easy access to information** – by using the metrics built in the crypto trading platform, a trader finds it easy to acquire information about an asset.
- **Depend on the supply and demand ratio –**

The fundamentalist relies on the demand/supply principles of economy. When the demand for a crypto is high, the price goes up. When the supply is low, the price also rises. The reverse is also true. In addition, the reasons behind the price movements are considered.

The demerits are:

- **Insignificant benefit** – There is no significant profit since major market movers hold the information FA relies on.
- **Relies on the skills of the analyst** – FA is a complex approach and its efficiency is dependent on the skills of the investor investigating the fundamentals. It is easy to commit analytical errors in the process.
- **Cannot pinpoint the best entry or exit positions** – it is not easy to determine a position quickly using FA.
- **Not suitable for short-term traders** – Since the analysis is conducted based on long-term trends, it is not ideal for short-term investments.
- The asset value is based on past financial results
- **Subjective** – it relies on so many assumptions.

For instance, it determines what an asset's worth should be rather than what it is.

- Time-consuming since qualitative analysis requires days or weeks to get better results.

To curb the risks fundamental analysis face, it is combined with technical analysis. A trader looks up fundamental indicators of an asset to establish an exit point and leverage technical analysis for an entry position. Alternatively, a trader may determine the exit position using a technical analysis, then leverage FA to verify the sell based on asset demand.

PUTTING IT INTO ACTION

Cryptocurrency being a new concept, finding reliable information has turned out to be a challenge. In comparison to traditional investments, analyzing cryptocurrency is a difficult task. Despite the speculations of the crypto market, doing a fundamental analysis is not impossible. For the record, there is no approved conceptual structure for conducting FA. Below is a list of factors that can guide analyzing crypto stepwise.

1. Find the market cap

Market capitalization refers to the aggregate value of an asset in the market. The market cap is important to show how saturated the market already is, i.e., considers the crypto supply to determine the potential for growth. Projects with larger market cap have lesser growth potential than those with lower market cap.

Market cap is calculated by finding the product of a cryptocurrency's current market price and circulating supply. A low-priced crypto could measure up to the level of a high-priced crypto in terms of market cap depending on its amount of circulating supply. However, it would have a low chance of growth since it would require significantly larger investments for its price to double. Thus, a crypto with a lower market cap has a great potential for growth than that with a higher cap.

2. Evaluate coin demand and supply

The value of an asset is determined by its demand and supply. The higher the demand and the lower the supply, the higher the value of the asset. Evaluate whether the usefulness of the token is sufficient to drive demand. When conducting fundamental analysis, consider these two principles of economy coupled with tokenomics and utility. Tokenomics refers to the economy surrounding tokens.

Also acknowledge the reversibility of the demand/supply law.

3. Determine liquidity and trade volume

How frequent is the asset traded? The trade volume reflects the recognition and adoption of a coin. It shows how much an asset has been sold and bought in exchanges. A cryptocurrency with higher trade volume shows that the crypto is in demand. Therefore, evaluate the trade volume of a cryptocurrency using major exchanges. If the currency is not listed on major exchanges, then avoid it. There is a reason why the exchanges want nothing to do with it.

4. Find the use case

What is the coin used for in the real world? Does it solve any real problem? Some projects pop up to benefit the team behind them without having a real purpose. Evaluate whether the project will realize its purpose in solving the problem. Check whether the network is sufficient to meet the obligations.

If the blockchain works to solve a problem that can easily be solved by non-blockchain networks, then its existence in the market is timed. Being in a team of professionals and friends with similar interests might help you in this process.

5. Investigating the network management

The management is simply the founders and a team of developers working behind a crypto network. Investigating the management helps you weed out fraudsters to con investors through Ponzi schemes and scams. There are several ICOs chipping out with promises that they barely fulfill. The projects later vanish with investments.

Evade projects with shady or anonymous founders. Take some time to read their interviews and conferences before making investments. If a blockchain has a great team of developers and founders, it is more likely to be successful.

6. Investigating the potential roadblocks

What are the regulations bound on the crypto? Is it legal or illegal? Consider the relationship the coin has with the law. If the crypto does not adhere to laws and regulations of a country, its pricing could go down. Consequently, take into account the scalability of the crypto. Can it operate in larger scales? Scaling is one of the prevalent issues that threaten the existence of most cryptocurrencies, Bitcoin and Ethereum included.

Alternatively, check whether it has a worthy adversary. The market is full of Altcoins emerging every day, making the competition stiff. Check how many competitors there are in the market. A stiff and close competition makes it difficult for a project to be widely accepted. Or else, what competitive advantage do they hold against their competitors?

7. Find the coin roadmap

Roadmaps are the blueprint of upcoming plans of where the project is headed. Study the plans and draw your conclusions. How ambitious is the plan to move the project forward? A good blueprint is normally detailed and clearly states what has been done, when it was done, what will be done, and when it will be done.

HELPFUL TOOLS

Cryptocurrency differs from the traditional investments like stocks due to the decentralization of crypto. However, fundamental analysis barely varies despite the difference in specifics. To accurately conduct fundamental analysis, the investor will require the necessary tools like statistics that determine the performance of the asset or company. Such statistics include: Earnings per share, price-to-earnings ratio, price-to-book ratio, price-to-sales ratio, etc. The statistics of crypto are obtained from surrounding factors that influence the asset's value. Such factors are the number of active users, key events, or simply qualitative and quantitative factors.

Earnings Per Share (EPS)

This tool analyses the profits of each investment. It looks at a portion of an asset's profit allocated to the asset's shares. In terms of traditional investments, it is calculated as follows:

$$EPS = Net\ income/total\ shares$$

EPS indicates the profitability of a crypto by considering what a rise in the profits could mean for the future of the asset. An unusual rise could mean that the market will soon recover to its normal price; or the asset is facing a serious condition that has forced a crypto to reduce the market price of its coin. It also takes into account the liquidity of the asset.

Price-to-Earnings Ratio (P/E)

P/E ratio is the amount the market pays for the worth of the asset's earning. In terms of stock, it is calculated as follows:

$$P/E = Market\ price\ of\ each\ asset/Company\ EPS$$

P/E ratio is used to determine whether an asset is overvalued or undervalued compared to its correct value. The lower the P/E ratio, the higher the earnings. Thus, more attractive to investors who look for greater potential for price increment. However, an undervalued asset shows more growth potential because its market price might increase significantly.

Price to Book Ratio(P/B)

This ratio illustrates how much an asset is worth compared to its book value. It is calculated by dividing the current value of a crypto by its book value. If the value is more than 1, then the market price is expected to grow significantly at a faster rate.

Price to Sales Ratio (P/S)

P/S ratio compares the total revenue of an asset to the cryptocurrency's market capitalization. This helps in realizing the performance of an asset. It is calculated as follows:

```
P/S ratio = Market cap/total revenue
```

13

LEARNING TECHNICAL ANALYSIS

GRASPING TECHNICAL ANALYSIS

Technical analysis can be described as a trading discipline employed by professional traders to examine investments and spot earning opportunities by analyzing quantitative information gathered from market price and volume movements. The technical analysis primarily focuses on changes in price and volume of an asset to ascertain its value, unlike fundamental analysis, which focuses on business results such as profit margin and sales.

Traders use technical analysis to determine how the interplay between supply and demand impacts an asset's price, volume, and volatility. In most cases, technical analysis is used to speculate an asset's short-term price using various charts and tools. Besides, it can enhance the analysis of a security's strong and weak points connected to the entire market or sub-sectors.

Traders can apply technical analysis to any security with trading history. This includes traditional securities such as stocks, commodities, currencies, and now digital assets such as Ethereum. It was first introduced by Charles Dow back in the 1800s alongside the Dow Theory. Afterward, many other researchers in different fields contributed to the Dow Theory concepts to solidify its viability. Today, technical analysis has massively evolved and includes many patterns and trends discovered through decades of research and work.

Technical analysis is attributed to the assumption that investors can use historical trading data of a cryptocurrency to speculate on the future price of an asset when effectively used together with other trading principles. Seasoned traders use both technical and fundamental analysis to make informed decisions when trading cryptocurrencies. The classical approach towards technical analysis hinges upon:

- Historical price movements help us determine what is likely to happen in the future. It does not tell us exactly what will happen but helps us estimate the probability.
- The new traders will tend to follow the trading

pattern of the previous group of traders.

- Investors can predict human market behaviors.

As such, analyzing past price movements, changes in volumes, patterns, and trends, and the prevailing price and volume changes can help us predict the prospective future prices of cryptocurrencies. As such, you can now sketch the trends and patterns on the chart to come up with a graphical representation of the possible direction the price action may follow.

How does technical analysis work?

The primary objective of using technical analysis is to profit from the market by observing and analyzing market trends. Technical analysis helps you determine the entry and exit positions without allowing emotions to deter decision-making.

Technical analysis has two primary variables: the time frame and the technical indicator that the trader proposes to use. Time frames used in technical analysis range from 1 minute to monthly or even annual spans. The most utilized timeframes by technical traders include:

- 5 - minute chart
- 15 - minute chart
- 1 - hour chart

- 4 - hour chart
- 1 - day chart

The trading timeframe a trader chooses depends on the trading strategy employed by the trader. For instance, day traders who close their position by the end of the day prefer short timeframes such as 5 minute or 15-minute charts. Long-term traders who hold their positions for an extended period tend to use bigger time frames like 4-hour, daily charts, or even the weekly chart. Price swings that take place within a 15-minute time frame might be very crucial to daily traders who are looking to take advantage of short-term price movements.

Nevertheless, that price swing might appear negligible for making long-term investment decisions. This can be easily illustrated by viewing a specific price action using different timeframes.

Candlesticks

Candlestick charts are the most commonly used to indicate the direction of the price action on a chart. Candlesticks began in Japan more than a century before the westerners came up with the bar, point, and figures chart. A certain Japanese by the name of Homma found out that although the price of rice was connected to the law of supply and demand, traders' emotions actively swayed the market.

Candlesticks indicate emotions by visibly displaying the extent of price swings using varied colors. Traders utilize these candlesticks to make trading decisions depending on the constantly forming patterns that help speculate the short-term direction of the price action. A candlestick indicates the price at which the market opened, high, low, and the day's closing price.

ANOTHER ANALYSIS?

Apart from technical analysis, there is another form of analysis popularly known as fundamental analysis. Fundamental analysis involves delving deep into the cryptocurrency's available information. For instance, you might evaluate the applications of a crypto asset, the number of users, or even the development team behind the project.

The primary objective of conducting fundamental analysis is to decide whether a particular cryptocurrency project is overvalued or undervalued. Afterward, you can apply the obtained insights to determine your trading positions.

Succeeding in crypto trading requires one to master a certain set of certain skills. After mastering technical analysis and trading strategies, one needs to learn how to conduct fundamental analysis to strengthen their trading position. Fundamental analysis in the cryptocurrency industry is a model of evaluating a cryptocurrency project and determining the intrinsic value of its native token.

Understanding the difference between technical and fundamental analysis

When evaluating the market, technical and fundamental analysis are the two main schools of thought. Investors apply the two techniques to research and predict the future prices of digital assets. However, these two approaches are different. The major difference between the two comes down to what is driving the value of a cryptocurrency.

Fundamental analysis looks at the project's valuation. This depends on the number of investors or users, the development team, and the project's overall value. Fundamental analysts are interested in the difference between a token's price and the prevalent market price. On the other hand, technical analysis is focused on an asset's price action and trading history. This helps fundamental analysts to determine the asset's supply and demand dynamics. As discussed earlier, trading patterns tend to repeat themselves because traders have a habit of making decisions in particular situations. Technical analysts are interested in the volume and price action only.

The argument over fundamental and technical analysis is combative. Adherents of either method of analysis often dismiss their counterparts but miss the key point that they can both have their place. Fundamental analysis is mainly preferred by long-term investors, while technical analysis is most effective for short-term traders like day traders or scalpers and market timing. The two approaches can be effectively used together to come up with medium-term and long-term price predictions.

Short-term price swings are determined by the dynamics of supply and demand, which are influenced by what typically happens in fundamental analysis. Public sentiment and the emotions of traders can only be evaluated using the market price and volume. Contrastingly, charts and price history cannot be used to tell whether a token is overvalued or undervalued and what its future value may be. Charts mirror past events, and their importance depreciates over time.

5 TECHNICAL ANALYSIS TOOLS YOU SHOULD KNOW

Crypto traders use technical indicators to understand better supply and demand dynamics in the market and market psychology. Generally, these technical indicators forge the groundwork for technical analysis. Key metrics like trading volume provide us with signs of whether the price will rise. As such, these indicators can be used by traders to identify purchasing and selling signals. In this part, we will learn about five technical indicators to add to your trading kit.

1. Relative Strength Index

The indicator plots recent price gained compared to recent price lost between zero and a hundred. The RSI levels help a trader to gauge the momentum and trending strength. The Relative Price Index has three major uses:

a) Overbought and Oversold indicator

When the RSI levels are above seventy, the asset is regarded as overbought, a sign that it can decline. The moment the RSI levels are below thirty, the asset is oversold and could start rising. The assumptions might be dangerous hence traders are advised to sell when the asset goes above seventy and drop below. The traders should also buy the asset when it goes below thirty and rise back above.

b) Divergence

When the indicator moves in a reverse direction from that of the price, the current trend is weakening. The weakening of the trend indicates that it could reverse anytime.

c) Support and Resistance Levels

When the trend is going upwards, an asset will often hold above the thirty levels and reach the seventy level. Similarly, when the trend is downwards, the asset will hold at the seventy levels and reach below the thirty levels.

2. Stochastic Oscillator

The indicator is plotted from zero to a hundred. It measures the current price comparative to the price range over some periods. When the trend moves upwards, the prices are expected to make new highs, while the prices are expected to be making new lows during the downtrend. The indicator is used in indicating the overbought and oversold levels. Prices levels at eighty are regarded as overbought, and those at twenty are regarded as oversold.

3. MACD

MACD stands for Moving Average Convergence Divergence. The indicator helps traders to determine the direction and momentum of the current trend. Moreover, MACD provides several trading signals. When the MACD is above the zero levels, the trend is going upwards, and when it is below zero levels, it is a downtrend. The indicator consists of the MACD line and the Signal line, which is slower. MACD line crossing below the signal line indicates a downtrend and an uptrend when it crosses above the signal line. A trader should observe which side zero is to decide the trading signals they will follow.

4. Average Directional Index

The indicator is used to measure the strength and momentum of a trend. When the Average Directional Index (ADX) is above the forty levels, the trend has a lot of directional strength, either downwards or upwards, depending on the price direction. The moment the ADX goes below twenty, it is considered weak. The ADX line is colored black, and the other two lines, DI+ and DI- are colored red and green, respectively. All the lines indicate the direction and momentum of the trend.

5. Accumulation/Distribution Line

The indicator considers the trading range for the timeframe and estimation of where close is considering the range. The indicator gives volume more weight when an asset finishes near the highs than when it finishes near the midpoint. The indicators line moving upwards indicates an uptrend while that moving downwards indicates a downtrend. The A/D also helps in observing divergence. If the indicator is dropping while the prices are rising, the trend is weakening and will reverse.

COMBINING IT WITH OTHER METHODS

Limitations of Technical Analysis

Although technical analysis indicators help a lot in trading, they have some limitations.

Mixed Signals

One of the indicators can show a purchase signal while another shows a sell signal. This makes the trader confused on which direction they should trade. Some traders try to use several indicators, moving averages, and patterns to overcome the limitation.

Accuracy

The indicators are used to forecast assets and give the possible entry and exit points. The prediction is not a hundred percent accurate; hence cannot guarantee a profitable trade. The stock may fall after the entry or rise after exit.

Biased Opinion

Technical analysts examining the same asset may have different views. Different analysts use varying analysis tools.

Overcoming the limitations

The following tips can help a trader to structure their swapping approach and overcome the technical analysis limitations.

1. A trader should create and write down fixed regulations on how they draw price action patterns.

2. An investor should know the patterns they are trading and the variations they observe between a recommendable and bad pattern.

3. An individual should know the tools and indicators they use without changing them anyhow.

4. One should avoid the hindsight fault and focus on the past setups.

5. A trader should know that entries aren't that crucial; rather, it is what happens around the entries that may break or make a system.

6. A trader should study each section of their system to avoid subjectivity since technical indicators are discretional.

7. One should fully comprehend the limitations of trading patterns.

TECHNICAL ANALYSIS TOOLS FOR BEGINNERS

Bitcoin and Ethereum continue rising as time goes by. This has brought huge benefits to altcoins which have started increasing their market value. A trader should take advantage of the Bull Run by adopting the following three tips:

1. Marking Important Points

The tip helps a trader to determine the levels where an asset might face resistance. This helps an investor to set accurate "Stop Loss" and "Take Profit" orders. Price candles have plenty of meaningful information. A red candle indicates the presence of strong sellers with a big wick above. A green candle with a big lower wick shows strong buying.

2. Zooming Out

Trading the trend on short time frames limits the investor's notion of the general trend. Zooming out aids a trader in determining whether the trend is upwards or downwards. Considering the current cryptocurrency bull-run, altcoins' prices rose, followed by a consolidation, then another exponential rally. The Defi tokens have been following the same direction.

3. Meaning and identification of Patterns

A trader should observe the price charts to understand the behavior of values in the crypto market. Patterns that repeat in different time frames develop frequently. The formation offers profitable trading opportunities. The most repeated chart patterns include; wedges, triangles, channels, bottoms, tops, and flags.

14

HOW TO MANAGE YOUR MONEY

T rading is profitable when done correctly. Contrary, when done wrongly, it can cause unimaginable losses. There are recommended trading habits which a trader should practice and make them their traditions. One of the habits is the Money Management Plan. Money in the financial markets is a valuable asset and should be handled carefully using Money Management Strategy.

TRADING IS NOT GAMBLING

Gambling is described as betting on something based on a contingency. In the trading field, gambling involves a more complex dynamic than presented by its description. Most traders gamble unknowingly by trading in a particular way or by trading for a purpose that is fully dichotomous with the market's success. The following are some of the hidden ways in which gambling enters into trading practices:

1. Social Proofing

Some individuals without interest in investing in the financial markets may find themselves trading due to social pressure. This occurs when a team of traders is discussing investing in the market, and the individual feels the pressure to conform to their social circle. The individuals either invest so that they are not left out or so that they don't disregard other members' beliefs. A trader can appease their social pressures if they have a solid investment comprehension.

However, traders gamble when they decide to enter the markets with no solid investment comprehension. The market consists of many variables, misinformation among the investors, and generation of gambling situations by traders. Until knowledge that permits traders to encounter the odds of losing is developed, gambling will continue occurring in every transaction that happens.

2. Contributing Gambling Aspects

When individuals indulge in the financial markets, there is a learning curve based on social proofing and may be viewed as gambling. The view depends on the trader's beliefs. Moreover, how the trader approaches the market judges if they emerge as successful traders or will continue being gamblers in the financial markets.

3. Gambling for Excitement

Losing trades can also cause emotions and a sense of satisfaction. This occurs mainly if the loss is associated with social proofing. If the traders in the individual's circle are losing cash in the market, losing money will allow them to participate in the conversation using their own experience. Individuals trading for excitement or social proofing mostly trade in a gambling style rather than tested methodologies. Trading in the marketplaces an individual into a worldwide network of traders who have varying opinions, backgrounds, and beliefs. Traders are systematically detracted from trading after they are caught up in the "idea" of trading.

4. Trading to Win.

Most traders trade to win but do not trade as per the system. A trader should trade systematically in any odds-based situation. Most individuals trade to win and do not find a reason to trade if they aren't gaining. However, there is a concealed detrimental flaw concerning the winning belief and trading. When individuals are only aiming to make a profit, they might be driven further away from gaining. Emphasize winning may make a trader continue holding bad positions since they do not want to admit they have lost. Traders should take losses when the situation indicates to make profits in most of the trades. Holding losing positions shows that the trader is now gambling and no longer considering relevant trading techniques.

IDENTIFY YOUR RISK TOLERANCE

The trading platform which an individual selects depends on several factors. Risk tolerance is one of the aspects. The suitable trading platform for an individual depends on their investment's goals and time horizon. The trading platform proactively schedules for the trader's level of risk tolerance. Traders would prefer a trading platform that reflects the risk levels they are comfortable with. Risk tolerance affects potential gains on investment at all levels.

What is Risk Tolerance?

Risk tolerance is the degree of variability in investment gains a trader is comfortable tolerating. It is a crucial element; hence traders need to practically understand their abilities and willingness to tolerate big swings in the value of their capital. There are plenty of risk tolerance evaluations that are accessible by traders. Surveys and questionnaires associated with risks are some of the assessments. A trader may also decide to review worst-case profits for several asset classes in the past. The information helps a trader determine the money they are comfortable losing if they experience a bad trading year.

Importance of Risk Tolerance

Understanding an individual's risk tolerance level is very important, especially when customizing a trading tactic that conforms to their needs. Risk tolerance enables a trader to invest in diversified asset allocation, which suits their investment objectives. Besides, risk endurance simplifies the trader's procedure of understanding their attitudes towards investing. The simplification helps the trader to forecast their possible reactions in future occurrences. Moreover, risk tolerance enables the trader to adapt their financial plan, concentrating on future occurrences that are real to their risk profile.

Factors that affect Risk Tolerance

1. Risk Tolerance by Time Horizon

Conventionally, younger traders have longer trading terms than older traders. Old traders, particularly the retired ones, have a low-risk tolerance. Traders should also consider other factors such as investment. Risk tolerance should be more conservative if the time frame involved is little. Longer time investments involve aggressive capitalizing. A trader should not follow traditional knowledge blindly regarding risk tolerance and asset categories. For instance, a trader in their sixties should not put all their capital into a conservative investment just because of their age. Conserving all the investments might be suitable for some traders since a trader in their sixties might have a twenty-year-old time frame.

2. The Risk Capital

An individual's net worth is calculated as net assets minus liabilities. Risk capital involves an investment of money that will not change the trader's lifestyle while lost. A trader with a higher net worth can take more risks compared to a lower net worth trader. Unfortunately, individuals with lower net worth are mostly involved in riskier investments due to the allure of quick and large returns. When a trader uses limited capital in higher-risk situations, they may get out of positions earlier than necessary. If a trader with limited capital uses defined risk instruments, they may recover from the loss quickly. However, a higher net worth trader may take a lot of time to recover if they had put all the capital in the risky trades.

3. Comprehending Your Investment Objectives.

The goals of an individual's investment should be considered when determining the risk they can endure. For example, if the trader saves their children's college fees, they should determine the risk they want to take using that capital. One can risk more if they are using disposable capital to get an extra income. One can use retirement money to trade higher-risk instruments if they have good trading futures and only use a part of their Individual Retirement Account funds. One should avoid taking a high risk if they have limited net worth and use their entire retirement funds to trade. Futures get favorable capital profits treatment hence a trader with limited capital should avoid taking higher risks.

4. Investment experience

Traders with less experience should avoid investing huge capital in higher-risk situations. Beginners should be cautious and indulge in trades that, even in the worst cases, they will be able to recover and continue with their lives.

YOU HAVE A PLAN

Deciding when to exit a trade can be tougher compared to deciding when to enter a trade. Lack of an exit tactic can make the trader take premature returns or unknowingly become an altcoin holder. A trader can adapt several exciting strategies to improve their money management in the financial markets.

1. Keep Calm and Close the Deal

Trade exit involves closing a deal either profitably or with a loss. An individual should develop a discipline of obeying their primary strategy exiting parameters. A trader should put their emotions aside, especially when trading cryptocurrencies. This is because, in crypto, a currency can skyrocket today and hit new lows tomorrow. New traders panic when the crypto asset swings in the opposite direction of their trade and end up closing the deal with losses.

Similarly, emotional traders may find themselves holding positions when after hitting their take-profit levels. Investors should set the time when they exit the trade even if they have not accomplished their desired returns. Different trading styles involve varying exit timeframes. Therefore, a trader should select the timeframe that suits their trading style.

2. "Take Profit" and "Stop Loss"

Taking profit and stopping Loss orders are the primary principles in trade exit. When an individual is trading, they should first ensure that the market trend is in their direction. The trader can then set their Stop Loss slightly below the support level and take profit slightly above the resistance level. Some individuals set their S/L and T/P at fixed values in every pair. This may lead to Stop Loss orders being executed earlier for high volatiles crypto or late for pairs swapped in a narrow range. When setting the orders, the risk-reward ratio should be around 1:2.

HOW MUCH CAN YOU TAKE

What is your maximum pain? Every trader should determine the maximum pain they can endure in case the trade goes south. Maximum pain theory came up with the "Max Pain" term. Max Pain is the price at which stock can cause financial losses for the biggest number of option holders at expiration. The maximum pain theory indicates that most investors who purchase and hold option contracts till expiration lose money.

Max Pain Understanding

The Maximum Pain concept explains that the principal stock's value descends toward its maximum pain strike price. Alternative writers hedge the agreements they have written while market maker performs hedging to remain impartial in the stock. A trader should consider the market maker's position if they have to write an alternative agreement without a stock position. Alternative writers tend to purchase or sell shares to drive the value toward a closing price that is favorable for them. On the other hand, call writers sell stocks to reduce the price and make holders purchase stocks to push the price up. The "maximum pain strike price" lies in the middle of the two. Approximately sixty percent of alternatives are traded, thirty percent expires with no value, and ten percent are exercised. The concept is regarded as controversial. The critics are divided into whether the tendency of the underlying stock's value gravitating in the maximum pain strike value is a case of market manipulation or by chance.

Max Pain Calculation

It is an easy calculation, but it consumes a lot of time. The calculation involves summing the outstanding put and call dollar price of each in the money strike price.

Procedure

- Find the difference between stock value and strike value
- Multiply the answer by open interest in that strike
- Add the dollar price for put and call in that strike
- Repeat the procedure for every strike value
- Find the highest value strike price= Max Pain Price.

Since the Max Pain price may change daily, using this as a trading tool is difficult. A huge variance between the stock price and the Max Pain value may be a tendency for the stock to move near the Max Pain. However, the impact of the move may not be meaningful till the approach of expiration.

DIVERSIFYING YOUR INVESTMENTS

Diversification serves the purpose of managing risks by combining a variety of different investment tactics. Every trader aims to create a group of investments that avails their portfolio in many areas, reducing the general risk of their investment. A trader's portfolio can withstand negative impacts without having to endure too much value in their portfolios. The portfolio should be well balanced to conquer the worst market crashes.

Importance of Diversifying Cryptocurrency Portfolio

1. Protecting against risk

This is the major advantage of diversifying cryptocurrency. Even if mitigation of crypto's risk is impossible, a trader can still reduce the impact volatility one asset will cause on their portfolio. An investor can achieve this by investing in different assets and incomes from stablecoins. Diversification lowers the risk of permanent loss because even if one asset crashes, others may be doing it differently.

Some of the assets might be rising while others might be holding, which places the trader in a better position.

2. Learn about different Coins and Projects

Nowadays, most traders are aware of Bitcoin and Ether assets. Traders should realize that there are other tokens available such as the CHSB. The other coins have different purposes and different financial performances over time.

3. Better Performance

Some traders may observe Bitcoin's bull-running and lack a reason for investing in other cryptocurrencies. Bitcoin also has huge crashes, which are remarkable. For example, in December 2017, Bitcoin's value dropped by forty-five percent in five days, from December 17th to December 22nd. The scenario pressures traders to have perfect market timing. Diversification offers stable profits, enabling traders to be more flexible in entering and exiting the market.

How to Diversify Your Investment

1. Industry Diversification

This diversification exposes the trader's portfolio to many industries. In a scenario where one industry incurs a huge loss, the trader's portfolio will encounter the loss. Examples of industries one can invest in includes medical, supply chain, data analysis, and finance. One can also diversify their investment by picking multiple projects in a certain industry. One should invest in industries in which they know about.

2. Type of Solution

An individual can invest in different kinds of products. One can spread their capital in newly developed blockchain platforms, protocols, and services; wallets. Investing in varying segments of blockchain markets enables an individual to spread their risk.

3. Cryptocurrency Type

A trader can decide that they only want to invest in privacy currencies since they see great potential in that area. Other areas a trader can invest in include stablecoins and utility tokens. An individual should analyze the varying possibilities and the way they will allocate their portfolios.

4. Geographical Diversification in Cryptocurrency

A trader should have different projects from all over the world in their "Crypto Diversification Portfolio." For instance, the Asian blockchain projects contain a huge and loyal following. This makes the project a recommendable investment alternative. The big and loyal following shows the extent of the project's success. A trader can decide to mix up the Asian blockchain project with other projects like Europe and America.

A trader can develop a money management tactic in cryptocurrency trading easily. However, the most difficult habit of adapting is personal discipline. Traders should practice personal discipline to be profitable investors.

15

IF NOT TRADE, THEN?

MORE THAN TRADING

There's more to cryptocurrency than just trading. With the advancement in technology, crypto is growing at an unprecedented growth, and it is offering real-time uses in the current market. Most people invest in cryptocurrency without knowing when and how to invest and, most importantly, where to invest their earned profits. Here are tips to help in doing more than trading with Bitcoin and altcoins.

One of the most fundamental ways to gain maximum returns is by buying and holding. It is common among cryptocurrency traders and is very safe, whereby a trader buys coins that have a chance of rising then hold them until a fair market price, and then they sell the coins. One can hold these crypto coins for months or years until a perfect market arises. Many peer-to-peer platforms allow a trader to lend cryptocurrency and offer a 12-18% profit of your investment in the form of Bitcoin. After buying and holding cryptocurrency, the next smart move to make a trader some profit would be to lend out their coins.

Investing all your savings in one cryptocurrency could be a risky affair. A trader may want to consider investing in other cryptocurrencies as they diversify their portfolio. One may invest in other coin projects to maximize on return. There are more than 50 cryptocurrencies launched every month; investing in an ICO (Initial Coin Offering) means optimum profit return because a trader buys a coin before its release date. As a trader, one may consider using brokers to thrive in the cryptocurrency market. A broker helps a client trade on a smaller market while maximizing profits, and there is nothing wrong with that.

Learn day trading in the crypto market. Day trading operates on how high a coin is in volatility and liquidity. Buying Bitcoin at low prices and selling them at high prices is the primary mode of trading which means you lose on many investment opportunities. Learn how to short trade because this comes in handy as the crypto market is very volatile.

As an investor, there is a need to be very comfortable with risk, and this adaptability is required if you are going to maximize your returns. Controlling risk and avoiding risk are two different concepts. In trade, without risks, there are no rewards, and this also applies in the crypto market. Having an investment strategy is highly advised, one that is highly concentrated on big winnings. It would be best if you took the profits to go due to the debate around for years on how illegal or legal the cryptocurrency is. The future of this trade is not well known; as a trader, one should make their profits as early as possible and move on to the next investment platform.

Cryptocurrency can be used to make payments for purchases (goods or services), which doesn't take much time. For example, a $99 million Litecoin transaction only took about two and a half minutes to process, and the transaction fees were fair. If this money transfer had gone through standard financial intermediaries, it would have taken more time, up to days, and the transaction cost would be a bit higher.

Jurisdiction laws have been known to play a hand in the freezing of assets for individuals as court proceedings go on, leaving a person with no money to live by. The good news about cryptocurrency is that it is decentralized, which means no one controls it. With private keys and a digital wallet, no government can freeze any crypto asset. Cryptocurrencies such as Bitcoin act as a censorship-resistant alternative to store personal and corporate wealth.

Cryptocurrency allows you to make private transactions without a trace. This is an added advantage from bank transactions where you can't make transactions without explanations and paper documentations. This unnecessary bureaucracy can be avoided by making transactions using crypto platforms, one can trade privately and any sum of money desired.

The explosive nature of cryptocurrency now makes it possible to travel the world and pay for vacations in cryptocurrency. Some established travel agencies allow payments in crypto to book flights, car rentals, flight tickets, and hotel and apartment accommodations. The availability of Crypto ATMs has allowed travelers to transform their cryptocurrencies to local currencies in most major cities in the world.

The Bitcoin luxury marketplace De Louvois enables the crypto-rich to purchase luxury materials such as Tesla and Private Jets. There are several fashion houses as well that have started to accommodate cryptocurrency as a mode of payment for their products. These marketplaces offer luxurious goods such as art, fine wine, and real estate, all fully paid for in cryptocurrency.

YIELD FARMING IN DECENTRALIZED FINANCE

You may ask, what is Yield Farming? Yield farming is the practice of staking cryptocurrency or lending crypto assets to generate high returns or rewards in additional cryptocurrency. Yield farming is currently the most significant growth driver of the still-nascent Defi (decentralized Finance) sector. It involves a trader lending out their cryptocurrency to others through a computer program called Smart contracts.

Liquidity mining occurs when a yield farming trader earns additional tokens as compensation. Tokens are made during trade, and one thing they have in common with all cryptocurrencies is that they are tradable and have a price, so if tokens are worth money, one can bank with them.

Most Popular Yield Farming Protocols

Yield farmers use a variety of different Defi platforms to optimize the returns on their staked funds. These platforms have typed in incentives and protocols. The launch of COMP-token is attributed to the growth of yield farming. Governance tokens grant rights to token holders; a common way to start a decentralized blockchain is to distribute these tokens algorithmically with liquidity incentives. This attracts liquidity providers to `farm' the new token by providing liquidity to the protocol. So, what are the most popular platforms that yield farmers use?

1. Compound Finance

Compound is an algorithmic money market that allows users to lend and borrow assets, and it's a platform where adjusted compound interest and the governance for tokens can be earned. With an Ethereum wallet, anyone can supply assets to the compound's liquidity pool and earn rewards almost immediately after compounding.

2. MarkerDAO

Maker is a decentralized credit platform that supports the creation of DAI, a stable coin algorithmically pegged to the value of USD. Interest acquired is paid in the form of a stability fee. Anyone can open a Marker Vault, where they lock collateral assets, and this debt incurs claims over time.

3. Aave

Aave is a decentralized protocol platform that practices lending and borrowing; interests are adjusted algorithmically based on the current market condition. Aave is also known for facilitating flash and quick loans and credit delegation, where loans can be borrowed and issued to borrowers without collateral.

4. Uniswap

It is a decentralized exchange (DEX) and automated market maker (AMM) that enables the user to swap almost any ERC20 token pair without intermediaries. Liquidity providers must stake both sides of the liquidity pool in a 50/50 ratio and, in return, earn governance tokens a portion of the transaction fee.

5. Balancer

The balancer is a platform similar to Uniswap and curve, but it distinguishes itself through flexible staking. It does not require lenders to add liquidity equally on both pools. Due to flexibility, it brings liquidity pool creation with varying token ratios.

6. Synthetix

It's a synthetic asset protocol that allows anyone to lock up stake or Ethereum as collateral and mint synthetic assets against it. Anything with a reliable price feed can be a synthetic asset. This practically allows any traditional financial asset to be added to the artificial pool of assets.

7. Yearn. Finance

Yearn. Finance is an automated decentralized aggregation protocol that allows farmers to use various lending protocols like Aave and Compound for the highest yield. This is useful for any farmer who wants a protocol that automatically chooses the best strategies for them.

The Risks of Yield Farming

Yield farming is complicated to some extent as it carries significant risk for both the borrower and the lender. Most profitable yielding farming strategies are highly complex and are recommended for advanced users and highly advised for those who have a lot of capital to deploy.

Yield farming is usually subject to high Ethereum gas fees and only worthwhile if thousands of dollars are invested as capital. Users also run the risk of impermanent loss and price fluctuations when the market is highly volatile.

Yield farming is also susceptible to hacks due to the vulnerabilities in Smart contract protocols. Due to the nature of Defi, some of the many protocols are developed by small teams and on small budgets; hence it increases the risk of smart contract bugs. Due to the volatility and unpredictable nature of blockchain, this can lead to the loss of user funds. The Defi ecosystem is highly dependent on each other protocol because the protocols can seamlessly and permissionless integrate. This means that the entire system is co-dependent on each other, and one mistake from one protocol affects the rest of the protocols, causing them losses.

INVESTING IN START-UPS

In start-up companies, opportunities lie in companies that offer conversions between cryptocurrency and local currencies. in the current market, these platforms are receiving plenty of interest from cryptocurrency users. There is an advantage to dealing with these companies because they accommodate real-life situations in trade and purchase goods and services.

Cryptocurrencies can be used in start-up companies from two angles. One would be from investors who want to invest with a company that takes crypto as payment. Secondly, it would be from business owners who want to start companies that want to incorporate cryptocurrency in their websites, accepting them as payments.

Fundraising and investment strategies are most important if you want to get benefits in the cryptocurrency market. Due to this reason, Bitcoin and other cryptocurrencies are making mainstream which helps start-up founders and investors to start their fundraising and investment plans. Here are ways you can use cryptocurrency to raise funding:

1. Launch an ICO

An ICO (Initial Coin Offering) involves creating a cryptocurrency people can buy with crypto or Fiat currency. As the company grows, investors hope for the growth of the token that they can use to make purchases and convert it into local currency. Unlike the IPO (Initial Public Offering), you don't have to share ownership with investors, and you can keep all the freedom of the company's management.

2. Create a new cryptocurrency product.

Cryptocurrency is lucrative for a start-up company; building a crypto product makes a trader more relevant among investors. In Q1 of 2019, companies raised more than $173 million in investments. To integrate crypto into your start-up successfully, you can build a blockchain platform, create your currency, or make an app that helps people stay updated with the current news in the cryptocurrency market.

3. Join a Crypto Accelerator

Crypto is highly popular among start-up owners; jumping on a new successful trend will help you network with investors and other business owners. Networking and attending crypto, events put you in a visible place to work with the best trendsetters in the market.

4. Encourage clients to pay with crypto.

If you are going to add crypto to your payment options, you need to be aware of both sides of what this means to your start-up. On one side, it will attract clients who are using crypto to your establishment, and on the other hand, it can turn away clients who use fiat currency. Yet again, cryptocurrency is very volatile, and its price can go down as soon as it comes up; you don't want to bet your whole investments on luck.

Cryptocurrency comes with its pros and cons, and to some extent, they come in equal measure. The start-up may be doing so well, and in the next minute, it is at the bottom of the barrel. This is due to the nature of cryptocurrencies; the risk in investing in start-ups involves the degree to which a platform will flop or thrive.

Before you decide on the process of creating and investing in start-ups, you may want to consider getting an analyst and a bitcoin financial advisor to walk you through exactly what needs to be done to be able to thrive in the cryptocurrency ecosystem.

CENSORSHIP RESISTANT ALTERNATIVES TO STORE WEALTH

Bitcoin offers freedom from political repression on finances, which is a great deal in financial independence. Freezing a bank account is easier than it looks or sounds; it just takes one whisper of financial misconduct or attachment to criminal activities, and their bank accounts and assets are frozen. Bitcoin is not a hot crypto investment movement; it has positioned itself at the core need of future generations. This is not good news to everyone as the government would want to defend its status quo on matters of financial security, as Bitcoin has been linked to terrorist organizations.

Censorship resistance as a foundation comes as an asset, one that cannot be stopped or confiscated by any government. Users' finances cannot be controlled by any other party but themselves; this includes the developers or miners. Due to the decentralization nature of cryptocurrencies, no outside player has authority over anyone's coins. Also, there are private keys when it comes to any transaction.

This program favors Bitcoin because its censorship program offers freedom from financial repression; secondly, it's emerging as a natural successor to gold as a store of value. Thirdly Bitcoin is available to hundreds of millions of users, so the market availability of merchants is supreme. Lastly, the Bitcoin community is devoted to making Bitcoin a notable currency.

Bitcoin censorship resistance is solid such that the government cannot throttle or monitor your financial transactions as they can typically do in the financial world. Countries like Nigeria, India, Belarus, China, and Russia are prone to economic oppression; these countries have heavily welcomed cryptocurrency trade because of the freedom in the crypto market. Governments tend to want to keep a close eye on their citizens regarding their financial status.

Censorship resistance is the critical property that gives cryptocurrency its value of importance. Without this property, we would theoretically term cryptocurrencies useless. It mostly has individual advantages, we can term self-cantered. On the other hand, this is a risky affair because of the repercussions of decentralization. Cryptocurrencies have been linked to terrorist organizations.

The main con of this platform is the increase in crime rates; they are funded with a very private system, and it is hard to build a criminal case or arrest culprits as there is no evidence to go by. This property blindsides the government when handling security matters as global crime syndicates can operate without a trace. Also, it's harder to punish criminals as they have money they can access in the form of Bitcoin.

Personal Use and Decisions

At the end of the day, it is a personal decision to use your crypto coins. Of the many options handed to you, it's up to you to decide how your investments benefit you. Maybe you want to concentrate on trade just by buying and selling or you want to take it to another level and business on other aspects of cryptocurrency.

The future of bitcoin is a bit frail, and at the same time, it has survival rates in the current world. Will it survive the test of time? Will governments get a hold of the system and centralize it? What is the future of fiat currencies? Can they co-exist at the same period? The answers to all the above questions will be worked out as time goes by.

In the meantime, Bitcoin and altcoins are the new financial grounds in the world, with a significant trend set already, and in the last few years it has grown at unprecedented speed. It is a field you may want to consider trading in or not.

Many debates are going on with a noticeable split among the top global financial influencers. In the end, my biggest question about Bitcoin is whether people are interested in it because it's Bitcoin or because it's worth a lot of dollars?

CONCLUSION: THE FUTURE

Cryptocurrency is a new topic in the global financial market, and it has attracted a lot of attention, and its future looks very promising and inevitable. A tweet sent out by Elon Musk on 29th January 2021, "in retrospect it was inevitable," was a game-changer; it sent Bitcoin on a surging rise and it gained significant global attention because of his endorsement, and now there's no going back.

The nature of cryptocurrency is that it is very volatile and operates on a decentralized system. Its system comes with many advantages and disadvantages; it all depends on the angle you look at it from. There are factors and factions of cryptocurrency that have made it hard to ignore. It has gained the required attention to the extent that some nationals have started issuing national cryptocurrencies.

The past has been flooded with fiat currencies until cryptocurrencies crept into the market, and it's here for the long run. The legality or how legal cryptocurrency is, is the main discussion among governments and private entities. In the meantime, nothing has been decided, and that is to mean trading continues as usual.

Before you begin to trade, you need to be well equipped with information on what crypto is, how it operates, what platforms it operates on, how cryptography operates, and its decentralized nature. Above that, you need to understand what crypto can purchase and where these purchases are made and what global entities support crypto.

It's good to note that before you begin the trade, you need to be cultured into the Bitcoin and Altcoins (alternatives to Bitcoin) world and be armed with enough research on how to thrive in the market. Understand that above trading Bitcoin; by buying, selling, and holding, cryptocurrency can do so much more. Information on this has been provided in this book at great length.

There is a sure way fiat currencies operate in the current world, and there's a way they have taken hold of the world as we have transacted with them for so long. That is the same path you pursue to understand how cryptocurrency works. It's best to note that the primary currency that it operates on is the US Dollar.

As in any other market, there are scams, and cryptocurrency is not an exception to this fact. There are fake coins, fake traders, and con persons when it comes to the cryptocurrency world. So, it's best advised that you learn how the cryptocurrency ecosystem works and equip yourself with knowledge surrounding it, keep afloat with the daily news, read articles, and work with traders who have done this before. Understanding trade psychology is an intelligent choice to enable you to earn more from your daily trade.

A few notable mentions are Yield Farming and day trading in cryptocurrency. These are the new trade fields that maximize trade returns; they are risky and, to some extent, tough to understand. This book will find enough concrete and reliable information that will help you debunk these mysteries in the crypto market. A little tip for you, understanding them will set you apart when it comes to trade, and also, if you are beginning to trade, you may want to lay off until you can understand how they operate and later engage in that trade.

All information you require is encompassed in this book all-around, yet, let us talk about the future of cryptocurrencies. As mentioned earlier on there are debates on its validity. Worth mentioning is that bitcoin and Altcoins have created online global attention that cannot be ignored. Day in day out, its influence is being picked by developed countries, developing countries, and third-world countries.

Bitcoin will survive the future of finance, and it's a trend that is here to stay. This is because its advantages are individually based, and this is an opportunity all people who would like financial freedom are aligning themselves to. Pros such as privacy in trade, censorship resistance from governments, control over one's finances, and fast transactions that take a lesser time to process and lesser cost will be among the many reasons Bitcoin will thrive.

There are ups and downs concerning blockchain that are not only technical but also political. Cryptocurrencies have been linked to terrorist organizations; they will face a hard time being regulated and accepted as genuine cash to serve the government's agendas. It makes solving crimes a bit more complex than in earlier years. Blockchain networks protect their users from hacks, and they provide security keys that allow for illegal trading on these platforms.

As we move into the third decade of the Bitcoin trade, it's no longer a matter of will Bitcoin thrive? Instead, the more severe notion is when will the rest of the world catch up to it? Very soon, the global decentralized cryptocurrencies have an excellent chance to replace the government-supported fiat currencies without question.

With that in mind, both sides are working to stay on top of the game. With the crypto market working tirelessly to make itself efficient and the governments trying to centralize it as they have done with everything else. Bitcoin will do to banks what emails did to post offices.

Dear reader, it is entirely your decision to join this trade or not. You have all the information with you at this particular moment. Investments and entrepreneurship are options that require serious thought, as they go against the usual status quo of how our lives should be aligned and coordinated. Since cryptocurrencies are here to stay, the bottom line is that we need to figure out more ways to keep them relevant and translate them into our day-to-day lives.

As of today, you can do more than merely trade coins; they have integrated themselves in every corner of online marketing and are slowly and surely moving to the physical ground. You can acquire goods and services, travel the world, afford luxury, start companies, and pay for travel with cryptocurrency. What more do you want? Because, yet again, blockchain cryptocurrencies can do just that!

Made in the USA
Monee, IL
13 December 2021